Your Life in the Palm of Your Hand

YOUR LIFE IN THE PALM OF YOUR HAND

The Hand Analysis System of Self-Discovery

♦♦♦

Kathryn Harwig

SPRING PRESS
SAINT PAUL, MINNESOTA

For information contact Palm Productions LLC, 33 4th Street NW,
Osseo, Minnesota 55369, 1-612-424-3733.

Printed in the United States of America

Publisher's Cataloging–in–Publication Data
Harwig, Kathryn, 1951–
    *Your Life in the Palm of Your Hand, The Hand Analysis System of
    Self-Discovery*
    Includes index.
    1. Palmistry.   2. Self-Discovery.   I. Title
133.6H
ISBN 0-9638822-0-1

To Gloria Harwig,
who always believed I could do anything,

and

to Emma Magsam,
my role model for believing in myself.

Contents

Illustrations

1

Getting Started

*T*he art of palm reading has been practiced
for centuries.

Unfortunately, it has been shrouded in mystery and
pursued mostly by those interested in the occult or the
"new age," or has been used as a party game and at carnival
sideshows. This traditionally has kept the study of hand
analysis from being taken seriously by most people. For
reasons I hope you will discover in this book, palmistry has
the potential for becoming accepted by serious, curious
people who want to understand themselves better.

I became interested in palm reading as a very small child. I
do not remember a time when I was not fascinated by the
prospect of examining a waiting
palm. I did not understand what I
was doing and had no training in
the subject. I simply had the feeling
that by looking at a person's hand I
knew that person better.

> Palmistry has the
> potential for becoming
> accepted by serious,
> curious people.

As I grew older, I occasionally studied the few books and
materials available on palmistry. I learned the historical
names for the lines and fingers, and enjoyed the attention I
received at parties when I "read" a palm. Still, I considered
palmistry to be a minor diversion with very little lasting

significance in my life. By the time I had graduated from college, married and launched a career in law, I had completely forgotten my romance with palmistry.

As a lawyer in private practice, I am often asked to speak to various groups on subjects such as wills, real estate and elder law. As I began to give seminars about these subjects, the organizers would sometimes look for lighter topics as well. Innocently, I volunteered the information that I read palms. Little did I suspect that this would soon carry me toward a new career and a completely different way of viewing life.

Since my reintroduction to palmistry, I have discovered that hand analysis is an amazingly accurate and effective tool for discovery of a person's character and life experiences. I have seen people transformed by the knowledge of their personality traits and history. After reading perhaps thousands of palms, I believe that hand analysis can be used by anyone to attain self-knowledge quickly and confidentially. While I do not see palmistry as a substitute for therapy or counseling, it can be an aid to the study of the self. Hand analysis can be used by anyone interested in knowing themselves more fully.

The most commonly asked question about hand analysis is not "Does it work?" but "Why does it work?" Most people, after experiencing a reading, cannot deny the accuracy of this look into their character. Still the question remains, "How can your life and character be so accurately reflected in your hands?"

I do not have a perfect answer to that question. I believe that a person's life experiences, beliefs, and character traits are noted throughout the body. More and more, the mind-body connection is demonstrated to be a factor in our lives, health, and psychological welfare. It is no longer disputed that your emotions can make you sick or aid in your recovery. It is also well known that the external events of life affect every part of your physical body. It is not such a leap of faith to imagine that these events are recorded on your hands.

It is clear that the lines of our palms change with our emotional state and as we age. If you examine the hand of a small child, you are unlikely to see many lines other than the three major ones. For example, it is rare for a child under the age of ten to have a fate line. The minor lines such as the fate line develop as we age and experience life. In old age, we often lose some of our lines. Particularly among elderly people who have memory problems, the lines of the hand begin to blur and fade away as their interests and memories do the same.

Despite popular opinion, the lines on the hand are not created by folding or usage. If they were, both hands should be virtually identical. One glance at your palms will show that your hands have two very different stories to tell. Learn to listen to them and you will be fascinated by what is revealed.

No one is certain how the lines on the hands are formed, or what causes these lines to change. The most likely explanation is that the lines are created by the nervous system. This explains a number of different phenomena, including the fact that during periods of intense emotional distress the number of minor lines on the hands increases dramatically. It is also said that electric shock therapy has a great effect on the hands, often causing meshing and breaks throughout the lines of the palm.

Perhaps someday hand analysis will receive the credibility I believe it deserves, and the answer to how it works will be discovered. Until that time, I am content to base my belief on my experience. I have seen the truly amazing correlation between the length of the fingers and the width and depth of the lines of the palm with character traits and life history. I encourage you to try it.

What I ask is that you take what you like and leave the rest. If my analysis of your hand or character does not feel right for you, ignore it. This is a tool for you to use to discover yourself. You should never hand your power away to someone else. You should not let anyone else tell you who you are. When you follow the instructions in this book you will be using hand analysis as a tool for knowing yourself. You are the only expert on you.

How to use this book
This book is not a fortune-telling tool. I don't believe that your fortune is pre-ordained and written in stone, and I do not believe that any device can accurately predict your future. This is a book for learning about yourself. I hope you will use this book to introduce yourself to yourself, perhaps for the first time. Knowing yourself is the key to life's ultimate success. It is impossible to get what you want out of life until you know enough about yourself to truly know what it is that you want—what it is that will actually bring you peace and joy.

Our lives have become so busy, and we are so burdened with our roles and other's expectations of us, that few of us take the time to figure out who we are and what we truly desire. This book is meant to help you do that in a simple and enjoyable fashion. Because you are looking at a physical part of your body, this method will help you overcome your preconceived ideas of your character, and perhaps reveal things to you about yourself which you have not considered before.

Hand analysis is not meant to dictate what will happen in your life. Rather, its purpose is to illuminate what *could* happen in your life. If you follow the instructions and work in this book, your future possibilities as well as your past experiences will be revealed to you. You will also be able to use this system to more fully know the others in your life.

Some of what you will learn about yourself may not be comfortable. All of us have character traits that we view as less than favorable. Still, knowing these things about ourselves then allows us to make conscious decisions about keeping or eliminating these traits. Things do not go away just because we pretend they are not there. What we don't face about ourselves will continue to surface in our lives.

This book has been arranged as a workbook. For this method to be truly effective for you, follow the lessons as they are arranged. It is important that you fill in the illustration or answer the questions first. By following the steps in order, you can avoid allowing your notions of your personality to color your interpretation of your hand analysis. You may be surprised at what you learn about yourself.

You are then asked to comment on how, or if, this analysis fits for you. Ask yourself if the analysis has the "ring of truth" in describing your personality and life. Search your memory for instances in which these issues have arisen in your life and remember how you responded. If the prescribed analysis fits, make it your own. If, after careful analysis it does not, discard it. You are the final determiner of your personality and your fate. I only ask that you seriously consider the possible truths that this method suggests to you.

Life is a process, and your palms are its road map.

Which hand do you read?

It is important to look at both hands to get a full picture of your personality. Your dominant hand is the hand that you use most often, and that is generally your strongest hand. If you consider yourself to be "right handed," your dominant hand is most likely your right hand. The only exception to this is the case in which your "handedness" was changed by a well-meaning parent or teacher when you were a child. If that is the case for you, you should consider your dominant hand to be the hand that you automatically use when you need strength and skill.

In rare instances, a person does not have a dominant hand. In that case, you must read both hands in order to fully ascertain your character and personality.

The dominant hand is the hand which reflects the destiny and character that you have created. Reading your dominant hand will show you things that have actually occurred in your life, your personality, and your character. It shows the sum of your experiences in life.

In contrast, your non-dominant hand shows your life as it could have been—your potential for this life. Look at your non-dominant hand to see your character as it might have been, unshaped by your life experiences.

It is fascinating to compare your two hands. Most people assume that their hands are mirror images of each other. Nothing could be further from the truth.

> Take a minute to look at the palms of each hand. Notice how different the lines are in each hand. Now, measure the length of your fingers on both hands and record them on the illustrations on pages ten and eleven.

If you are like most people, you will find that your hands are very different. This is because the life that you have experienced has shaped and been reflected more on your dominant hand than on your non-dominant hand. Thanks to this phenomenon, you can see not only your current character and experiences, but also your potential and possibility, laid out for your enlightenment on the palms of your hands.

Another common belief is that the lines and features of palms remain unchanged throughout life. Again, this is false. Your life experiences and attitudes become imprinted on your hands, waiting for you to interpret them. As your experiences and life play out, your hands and lines change to reflect these occurrences. If you read your palms every six months, you will clearly witness these stories unfolding. Life is not static and neither are your hands. If you change your life, attitudes, and character, you will change your hands as well. Lines lengthen or disappear, fingers straighten or curve. Life is a process and your palms are its road map. Learn to read this map, and you will better negotiate the hills and valleys of your life's journey.

Before proceeding further, it is time for you to get to know your hands. Pages ten and eleven contain illustrations of right and left hands for you to fill in with measurements taken of your own hands.

Start by looking at one hand, palm side up, and examine your fingers. You will see that each of your fingers consists of three sections which are called phalanges (see Fig. 1). You can only clearly see your phalanges on the palm side of your hand. Most fingers have several lines at the bottom of each phalange.

With a small ruler, measure each phalange of each of your fingers, measuring from the bottom line of one phalange to the bottom line of the next. You will get a more accurate measurement if you measure in centimeters. After obtaining an accurate measurement, enter that measurement in the corresponding space on the sample hand. For example, if the top phalange of your thumb is three centimeters long, you should write three centimeters in the top phalange of the thumb in the illustration. When you have finished measuring all of your phalanges on both hands, you should have a number written in each phalange of the sample hands.

The total length of each finger should equal the total measurements of the three phalanges. Accuracy is important here, so take several readings to get as exact a measure as possible. After measuring all your phalanges and entering their length, measure the total length of your fingers and enter that figure in the appropriate space. Finally, measure the width of your palm at its widest point and enter that measurement also.

Phalanges

Fig. 4 shows the fingers labeled with their historical palmistry names. For ease of description I will use these names throughout the book. Try to become familiar with these names, as we will refer to them over and over again.

Congratulations! You have completed a time-consuming and somewhat difficult task, and have taken a large step toward learning to know yourself. Now it's time for some fun.

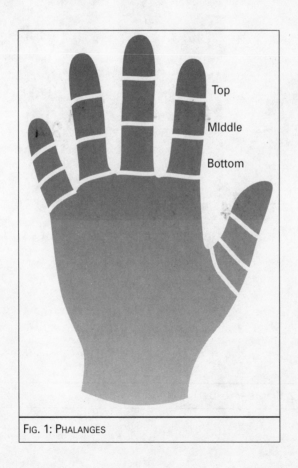

Top

MIddle

Bottom

FIG. 1: PHALANGES

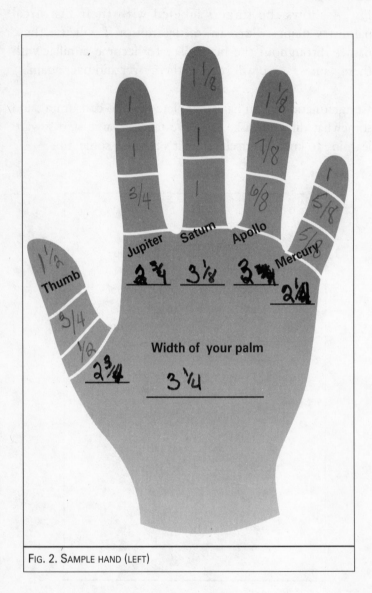

FIG. 2. SAMPLE HAND (LEFT)

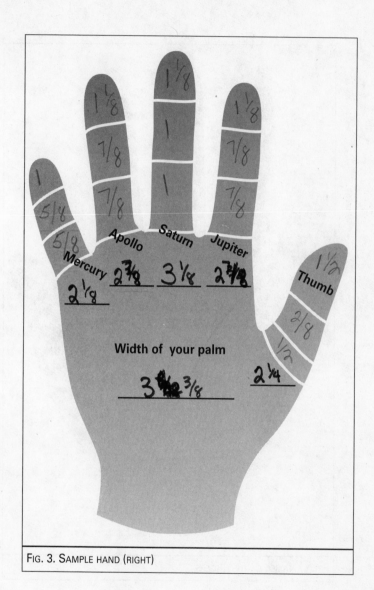

FIG. 3. SAMPLE HAND (RIGHT)

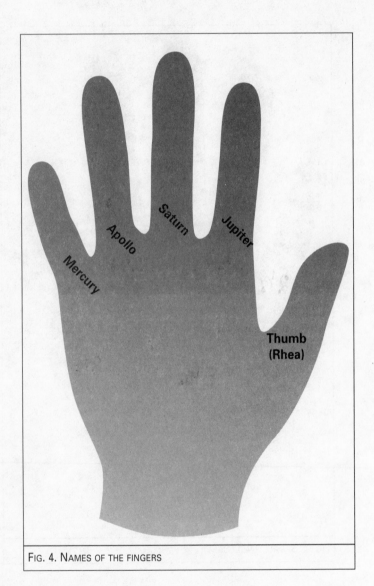

FIG. 4. NAMES OF THE FINGERS

2

Shape, Texture and Color

Before you learn the meaning of the length of your fingers and phalanges, examine your palm for its color, texture and shape. Look at the following questions, then answer them as accurately as you can.

What is the normal texture of your hands? Are they very dry and rough? Are they smooth and soft? ✓

How would you describe the color of your palm? Is it best described as red, pink, yellowish, white, or blueish? (You are looking for a definite yellow, red, or blue tint. If these colors aren't readily apparent, your hands are probably pink.)

How would you describe the usual temperature of your hands—hot, cool, cold?

 cool

In relation to the size of your hand and palm, do you consider your fingers long or short?

 long

Are your fingers better described as smooth or knotty? (See Fig. 5 for an example of a knotty finger)

smooth

Look at your nails. What color are they? Do they have ridges? Are the ridges horizontal or vertical?

Hold your right hand out in front of you in a normal fashion. Do you normally hold your fingers close together or are they splayed widely apart?

apart

Do you consider your hand and fingers to be flexible or somewhat inflexible? Do they bend and flex easily or are they somewhat rigid?

flexible

Now that you have answered these questions, review the following analysis for clues into your character and general health. Compare the following information with what you have gathered from examining your own hand.

Texture

Excessively rough, dry skin often indicates an eating disorder. Anorexics and bulimics frequently have extremely dry, flaky hands which are cool and sometimes clammy to the touch. Even people without blatant eating disorders can have very dry skin. If you have the type of dry, flaky hands which show no improvement with lotion or other products, you may be suffering from a vitamin deficiency. You should consider supplementing your diet with Vitamins C and E.

If you have very smooth, soft hands, you are probably quite concerned about nutrition and eat well-balanced, healthy meals. As a person with very soft skin, however, you may be a person who pampers yourself in all ways. You are seldom interested in exercise and you may be somewhat self-indulgent in regard to your body. Those of you with extremely smooth, soft skin may have a tendency toward narcissism and are often quite self-centered.

Color and temperature
The temperature and color of your hands tell a great deal about your physical health. People with warm hands usually have good physical health and high energy. Your hands are usually a pale shade of pink.

People whose hands are hot are those with a large amount of physical energy and stamina, who live life with high intensity and vigor. Your hands tend to be a brighter pink or red in color.

Cold-handed people tend to withdraw into themselves and do not open themselves up without coaching. If your hands are very pale pink, you are healthy. However, white hands are a sign of physical exhaustion.

Yellow hands indicate little energy and a possible liver problem. These are people who have poor immune systems who also have a tendency to suffer from depression.

Blue-tinged fingers indicate circulation problems. When your fingers are very blue, it may be a sign of significant heart ailments that should certainly be looked at by a physician.

Perspiring hands are not only a sign of nervousness and tension, they are the sure sign of a worrier. In addition, if, your palm contains a great many small secondary lines, it is a sure sign of excess worry and tension.

Length and smoothness of fingers

The length of the fingers is judged in relationship to the size of the hand and body and must be viewed in comparison to them.

> Looking at your measurements on pages ten and eleven, compare the width of your palm at its widest part to the length of your Saturn (middle) finger. If your hand's width is within one centimeter of the Saturn finger's length, your fingers are of average length. If your Saturn finger is more than one centimeter shorter than the width of your palm, you have short fingers. If your Saturn finger is more than one centimeter longer than the width of your palm, you have long fingers.

In general, longer fingers belong to more contemplative persons, with short fingers belonging to more impulsive persons. Knotty fingers, with pronounced joints and waists above and below the joints, are signs of great thinking ability, and belong to the academics and inventors of this world. Such fingers usually indicate that you have a vivid imagination with a tendency to be over-absorbed in work. This is the hand of the absent-minded professor. While oftentimes brilliant, those of you with knotty fingers tend toward cautious behavior and may never actually put your ideas into practice. It is almost as if the knottiness of the knuckles impedes the energy and causes caution.

If your fingers are short and knotty, you have the impulsiveness of the short-fingered person combined with good thinking ability. This is a very good sign for someone in a job that requires quick thinking such as police officer or salesperson. If you have long, knotty fingers, you ponder action for a long time before making a move. You are better suited for jobs involving research, teaching, or ministry.

Smooth fingers belong to impulsive people who often act first, think second. People with very smooth hands, like most children, are very likely to jump into things without fully thinking them through. You have a childlike view of the universe that can be both delightful and frustrating. A knotty-fingered person will find it difficult to keep up with a smooth-fingered friend, and the smooth-fingered thinker will find a knotty companion frustratingly slow. Nonetheless, if each of you is aware of your own and one another's method of acting, you make a good combination in getting work done.

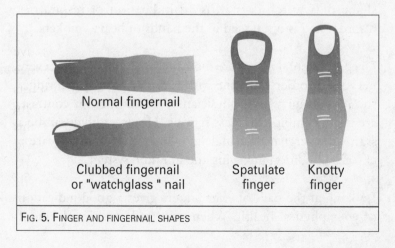

Normal fingernail

Clubbed fingernail or "watchglass" nail

Spatulate finger

Knotty finger

FIG. 5. FINGER AND FINGERNAIL SHAPES

Short, smooth fingers are a sign of one who occasionally acts without thinking at all. You are often impatient with those who want to think things through. You rely a great deal on instinct and intuition. You are good at jobs that require fast response with little or no forethought.

If you were looking to hire a person who can act quickly but who also thinks things through before acting, you would look for a person with long, smooth fingers. This person is not impulsive, just able to grasp things quickly at an intellectual level and act upon that knowledge, and would make an excellent lawyer, politician, or doctor.

Nails

Spatulate fingers are wedge-shaped with the nails splaying out wider at the top than at the cuticle. Despite being somewhat unattractive, they are a sign of artistic temperament, and indicate a person with a flare for aesthetics and a good eye for color and design. You will often see spatulate fingernails on the hands of artists and design professionals.

A *watchglass* nail, so named because it curves out in the shape of a watch crystal, is an indication of respiratory disorder and is often seen in the hands of heavy smokers.

Deep horizontal ridges are indications of infection or severe nervous disorders. Anyone with very deep horizontal ridges should consult with a physician. Vertical lines, in contrast, are more common and less serious. However, they can be a sign of several nutritional imbalances, or can indicate a chronic condition involving the immune system.

Looking at the nails of your fingers gives a good indication of your physical health. When your nails are tinted blue it indicates a lack of oxygen. This is why the anesthesiologist watches the color of your nails so carefully during surgery. If your nails have a blue tint, you may have circulation or heart problems and should certainly consult your doctor about this.

Broad, smooth, pink nails are an indication of physical health. Ridges in the nails often indicate a lack of vitamins and a sign of imbalance in the body.

People with bright red nails have a tendency toward having high blood pressure problems. You are often highly excitable with a propensity for having a quick and volatile temper.

White spots on a nail indicate stress and anxiety and are often seen on people with a tendency toward depression. These spots can also be a sign of a calcium deficiency.

A medical consultation is a wise decision whenever your nails show signs that are out of the ordinary. Many doctors regularly examine nails as a diagnostic procedure.

Position
How you hold your hand for analysis means a lot.

> Hold your hand in front of you in a normal, comfortable fashion. Are your fingers very close together or are they spread widely apart?

Fingers clamped tightly together indicate that you have a secretive nature. If you normally hold your fingers very closely together, it is likely that a part of you feels uncomfortable about self-revealing, even to yourself. It is wise to honor this part of yourself, and to take this program slowly until you feel comfortable learning new insights into your character and behavior. Remember that it is not necessary that you share this information with anyone else. There are many positive things about being hesitant to self-reveal. However, there is not much point in hiding your true nature from yourself.

If you spread your fingers widely, you are much more open and self-revealing. You are likely to want to share all of your new insights into your character with the world. You may wish to think a bit more carefully about all of this self-disclosure. Self-revealing people are easily hurt when others use this knowledge in hurtful ways or, perhaps, simply are not interested. While you should not stifle this delightfully open part of yourself, you may wish to self-reveal with a tad more discretion.

Many doctors regularly examine nails as a diagnostic procedure.

Flexibility

Take a moment to check the flexibility of your hands and fingers. Can you rotate your thumb freely? How far can your fingers be bent away from your hand? How wide can you stretch your fingers?

Flexibility of the thumb and fingers echoes flexibility in your life. In a highly flexible hand, the fingers can be bent far away from the hand. This indicates a very open mind, but can be taken to the extreme where you become overly compliant and wishy-washy. In contrast, the inflexible hand is found on a rigid and uncompromising person. If your hand is highly inflexible, you can loosen up your personality by loosening up your hand. Exercising and stretching your hand and fingers results not only in more mobility to your hand but more flexibility to the brain. Notice how, as people become older, they often become more rigid in both mind and body. Like everything else, this personality trait is written in your palm.

Of course, if your inflexibility is caused by some physical ailment such as arthritis, then it simply means that you have arthritis. As in all of life, a certain amount of common sense is required in hand analysis. For example, you will learn that fingers bent in a certain way indicate certain imbalances in your life. Do not forget, however, that if your finger is crooked because you broke it, then the meaning of its crookedness is only that it has been broken.

If your hand is highly inflexible, you can loosen up your personality by loosening up your hand.

Now, write what you learned about yourself in this chapter.

What does the color of your hand and nails tell you?

_____

_____

What does the texture and knottiness or smoothness of your fingers say about you?

Able to grasp quickly + act

_____

Are your fingers long or short? What does this mean?

long - contemplative

What is the normal temperature of your hand? What does this mean?

How do you normally hold your hand? What does this tell you?

apart - open - self revealing

What does the flexibility of your fingers say to you?

generally flexible in life

Does this seem true to you? Why or why not?

_____

_____

_____

_____

_____

_____

3

Thumb

*I*n palmistry, the thumb represents one's soul. The thumb (also called Rhea), is an extremely important finger on your hand. It has been said that possession of the thumb is the major factor that distinguishes people from the other living occupants of our planet.

Phalanges

All of your fingers are divided into three sections which are called phalanges. On your thumb, these three phalanges, from the top down, represent your will, your wisdom and your capacity to love.

Consult the measurements which you made of your thumb earlier and entered on pages ten and eleven.

Which is the longest phalange on your dominant hand (top, middle or bottom)?

Which is your longest phalange on your non-dominant hand?

The basic elements of your thumb (will, wisdom and love) should ideally be in harmony with each other. This means that the three phalanges would ideally be equal in length. Of course, this is not true in most hands. By measuring your phalanges you can determine which of these elements is most likely to control your life.

If the top phalange of your thumb is your longest phalange, you are likely to occasionally feel out of control. This is because your will is running your life. You will sometimes act without fully thinking through the consequences. Very long top phalanges belong to people who like to dictate to others—thus the term "under my thumb." If you run into a person with a very long and large thumb (particularly the top phalange), you should beware that this person may have the personality of a dictator.

Persons whose middle phalange is much longer than the other phalanges are good thinkers but not necessarily good doers. They make lofty plans and dreams that often never come to fruition. You may know people who have an opinion on every topic and a solution to all the world's problems, yet never take any action to address their own issues. These are people whose middle phalange is out of balance.

The bottom phalange of the thumb relates to your love of sexuality and sensuality. An overdeveloped bottom phalange may indicate a tendency toward excess in sex, food, or luxury items. If this phalange is much longer than your other two phalanges, you may wish for material things and luxury without either having the drive or having a plan with which to get these things.

Length of thumb

The total length of your thumb also tells a great deal about you. The length of your thumb can be compared to the rest of your hand by holding it close to the Jupiter (index) finger and then drawing a line to that finger.

Hold your thumb next to your Jupiter finger. Where does it reach on your Jupiter finger, i.e., middle of bottom Jupiter phalange, top of bottom phalange etc? Describe where it reaches:

middle

A thumb of normal length will reach the middle of the bottom phalange of the Jupiter finger. If your thumb is shorter than a normal thumb, it is an indication that you need additional motivation to achieve your goals in life. You have lots of good ideas but you often need "a kick in the pants" to get you going. You have a tendency to be impulsive, and you have been known to change jobs and relationships often without clearly thinking through the consequences.

A person whose thumb is longer than average is highly motivated and productive, although sometimes to the point of annoying and irritating others. You may be considered pushy and demanding. Working with you will be challenging but can also be frustrating. If you live or work with such a person, be prepared to learn the word "no." If you don't, you may find yourself over-worked and resentful.

Position of thumb

How you hold your thumb is also a good indication of certain character traits. Once you have learned these indicators, you will find that you are able to recognize many personality signs in others just by a glance at their hands.

People who conceal their thumb in their hands are afraid of revealing themselves to others. If you are meeting with a person who wraps the fingers around the thumb while speaking to you, you can be assured that this person will be slow to reveal his or her true self to you. This is also true of the person who holds the thumb close to the hand when the hands are at rest on a table or in the lap. You can be sure that you are dealing with a person who is afraid to be open, who is cautious, and who is unwilling to reveal himself or herself. Such a person will not appreciate being pressured to do so before he or she is ready. You should take things slowly with this person as she or he will not want much self-revelation from you either.

When a person holds the thumb far away from the rest of the hand, it is a sign of an adventurer who is anxious to take on the world. You will be impetuous and have a tendency to get yourself into trouble by acting before you think. You may very well tell more about yourself than others wish to know.

How do you normally hold your thumb? You may need to observe yourself over a period of days to determine this.

_____

_____

Mobility of thumb

The mobility of the thumb is a measure of your flexibility as a person. This mobility can be ascertained by checking the rotation ability of your thumb.

> Gently move your thumb in a circle and measure the ease of its movement and the size of the circle.

Your thumb is inflexible if it cannot rotate freely and cannot be held at a 90 degree angle to the index finger.

A very loose thumb indicates that you are easily swayed by the world and risk being influenced by others to too large an extent. You could be one to join cults and clubs without thinking through the consequences. You often have somewhat low esteem as to your own judgment and often value other people's opinions more than your own.

People with a stiff thumb are somewhat inflexible and stubborn. While you highly value your own opinion, you do so at the risk of not listening to others. You are sometimes accused of closed-mindedness.

Persons whose top phalange of the thumb bends far backward are often not interested in worldly things. You may be very self-sacrificing, perhaps to the extent of being self-destructive.

How you hold your thumb and the flexibility of your thumb is a factor that can be changed. If you feel that you are somewhat closed-minded and stubborn, perhaps it is best not to be perversely proud of this fact, but rather to work on loosening up your thumb. If you know that you lack confidence and do not self-reveal, you can practice

holding your thumb at a wider angle, and consciously avoid
hiding your thumb in the palm of your hand.

> What is the mobility of your thumb, highly flexible,
> loose, stiff? Again, you may wish to observe yourself
> over several days to decide this factor.

Mount of Venus

The fleshy part directly under each finger is called a mount.
The mount under your thumb is named the Mount of
Venus after the goddess of love. An average mount is
slightly fleshy but not overly puffy or bulbous. If you have
little or no padding at the area where it is normally fleshy,
you have a flat mount. If you have a great deal of padding
or puffiness, you have a bulbous mount.

> Look at your Mount of Venus. Would you describe it as
> flat, fleshy or bulbous?

A person with a thumb with a very bulbous Mount of
Venus will have a great love of life and its pleasures. You
may tend to eat or drink too much. You will have a great
deal of appreciation for the finer things in life, but may
tend toward gluttony and greed.

A very underdeveloped or flat Mount of Venus is often
found under the thumb of a person who doesn't have the
capacity to enjoy life's gifts. You are a person who cannot

appreciate the beauty and comfort of a decorated home, and does not savor fine foods. You may appear dour and unhappy to a connoisseur of such things.

Shape of the thumb
Fig. 6 shows some common shapes of the thumb.

> How would you describe the shape of your thumb, i.e., waisted, straight, bulbous, flat?

A very waisted thumb is a sign of diplomatic behavior, but can also indicate a manipulative person. You will be tactful and sensitive. However, if you run into a person whose thumb has a pronounced waist, it is wise to hold onto your wallet and your heart.

A very bulbous thumb with a deep-set nail has been called the murderer's thumb. It is found in people who possess violent impulses and have a great deal of energy with no natural outlet. This type of thumb usually indicates a tendency toward pronounced rage that is unexpressed. If you have a strongly clubbed thumb, it would be wise to examine your inner feelings of rage. Anger is an appropriate emotion when expressed in the correct way and time. Held in and unexpressed, this rage can explode. Therapy can be of great value in these cases, and clubbed thumbs can actually be reduced in size.

A flat thumb is one which has little or no cushioning on the fleshy part of the top phalange. Having a very flat thumb is a sign that a void exists in your life. You may feel drained and exhausted. This type of thumb is often seen in a person

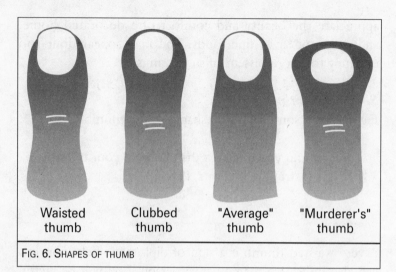

| Waisted thumb | Clubbed thumb | "Average" thumb | "Murderer's" thumb |

FIG. 6. SHAPES OF THUMB

of advanced age or in someone who has been very sick. Upon regaining your health, your thumb will often "fill out" once again—another sign that your hand changes as your personality changes.

Write a brief summary of what your examination of your thumb has told you about yourself.

Which is the longest phalange on your thumb? What does this tell you?

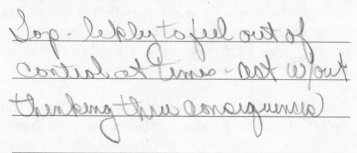

Top - likely to feel out of control at times - act w/out thinking thru consequences)

Where does your thumb reach when measured against your Jupiter finger? What does this say to you?

Middle - normal length

How do you naturally hold your thumb? What does this mean?

Away from hand - open

How mobile is your thumb? What does this mean?

flexible - open but not easily swayed - trust own judgement

What does your Mount of Venus say about you?

Avg. appreciate beauty and finer things in life

Does the shape of your thumb tell you anything about yourself?

Waisted - diplomatic

Does this seem accurate to you? In what way?

4

Jupiter Finger

The Jupiter finger is the finger of leadership, ambition, and ego strength.

Length

The name given by palmists to the first finger next to your thumb (sometimes called the index finger) is the Jupiter finger.

The key word to remember in describing the Jupiter finger is that it symbolizes your ambition, particularly in regard to career aspirations. Its length will show your hunger for power and success.

Returning to pages ten and eleven, compare the length of your Jupiter finger to the middle (Saturn) finger directly near it. It may help if you hold the fingers close together to compare them also. Where does your Jupiter finger reach on your Saturn finger, i.e., middle of top phalange, bottom of the top phalange, etc? Exact measurements are important here as a few centimeters can make quite a difference in meaning.

An average length Jupiter finger should reach the center of the top phalange of the middle (Saturn) finger. A normal length Jupiter finger belongs to those who possess a healthy form of ambition. You are anxious to achieve a high level of success and ambition in your career, but you are not so driven that you allow this urge to get in the way of other aspects of your life. Possession of this length of Jupiter finger reveals a balanced use of power, ambition, and leadership. In relationships, you would be confident enough to make a commitment without dominating the other person.

A person with a shorter-than-average Jupiter finger (one which does not reach the middle of the top phalange of the Saturn finger) often has a lack of self-confidence and a fear of failure. You tend to remain anonymous and avoid the limelight. You often have difficulty making decisions. You make a good employee and a good consultant as long as you are not expected to do something out of character such as public speaking. You function well with a strong partner. However, in a relationship you will try to give up your personal power to your partner who will end up making all the decisions. You will be loyal but dependent, and will look to others for your self-esteem. Short and long Jupiter fingers are often coupled in relationships, but usually with rather co-dependent results. In the extreme, this is a perfect prescription for a battering relationship.

If your Jupiter finger is longer than the middle of the top phalange of your Saturn finger, you have a tendency toward arrogance and egotism. Very long Jupiter fingers often accompany fanatical behavior and are found in some powerful religious and political leaders. This type of long finger has been called the Finger of Napoleon and indicates someone who may be a dictator. If you work for a person with a long Jupiter finger, you will find yourself under the rule of a domineering and aggressive boss—with an exaggerated sense of self-importance. If you are married to this person, you run the risk of being dominated in your relationship. These people can overwhelm you and you may feel that you are being swallowed up or engulfed in their personal magnetism.

Curved Jupiter finger

Look carefully at the Jupiter finger on your dominant hand. Is it straight or does it curve toward the Saturn finger?

curved

_____

If you have a curved finger, look at your non-dominant hand also. Is your Jupiter finger crooked there also?

yes

_____

A long, curved Jupiter finger (drawn to the Saturn finger) indicates that your ego has been submerged by authority or circumstance. I often see this in women who have been forced by society to give up leadership roles and responsible careers. If placed in a position where they can use their natural leadership capacity, their Jupiter fingers will straighten out to a large extent.

A short, curved Jupiter finger shows that you have been forced into a role that you don't want to play. This is often seen in persons who are forced to be more dominant than their basic personalities reflect. If your Jupiter finger on your dominant hand is crooked, you should check to see if your non-dominant Jupiter finger is also crooked. If it is not, it is a sure sign that you are playing a role which doesn't fit your inherent personality. You are trying to live up to someone else's expectations, perhaps a spouse, parent, or employer.

Most of the time, the Jupiter finger is curved or crooked only on the dominant hand. This is a sign that the forces of society have caused the imbalance. If your fingers are crooked on both hands, then the imbalance or difficulty is inherent in your character. It is more difficult to correct an inherent trait than one caused by societal forces.

Mount of Jupiter

Look at the mount immediately below your Jupiter finger. Is it flat, well-rounded, or bulbous?

The Mount of Jupiter indicates your level of resilience. A bulbous mount belongs to a person who bounces back strongly from disappointment, perhaps is almost incapable of permanent setback or insult.

A flat or even concave mount would indicate that you do not deal well with disappointment. You tend to give up in time of trouble or become severely depressed. It will take a lot of time and support for you to return to yourself after a difficult trauma.

Take some time to write out what you have learned about yourself through your examination of your Jupiter finger.

Is your Jupiter finger average length or is it shorter or longer than usual? What does this say about you?

longer - fanatical behavior -
domineering - aggressive -
dictator

Is your Jupiter finger curved? If so, is it curved on both hands? What does this tell you?

Curved on both hands - ego
Submerged by authority -
inherent trait - not by
anxiety

Describe your Mount of Jupiter. What does this mean?

avg - able to bounce back from disappointments

Does this give you any new insight into your leadership ability, ego strength and ambition? Does it seem right to you?

5

Saturn Finger

*T*he Saturn (middle) finger is the finger of balance
*and wisdom. This finger shows your capacity for
discretion, prudence, and planning.*

Saturn is the finger against which the other fingers are
measured. As such, it is not really long or short, except in
comparison to the others. It therefore does not so much
symbolize a trait as it acts as an anchor to the rest of the
hand and its traits. Losing the Saturn finger would cause a
person to feel drastically out of balance and out of touch.

Length

Returning to pages ten and eleven, examine the length
of your Saturn finger. How much longer is it than its
two neighboring fingers? Are the Saturn fingers on
both of your hands the same length? If not, which
hand has the longer finger?

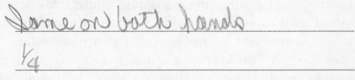

Same on both hands

¼

The Saturn finger should always be a fingernail longer than
the other fingers to indicate a well-balanced life. A person
with a long Saturn finger is morally grounded and balanced.

A shorter finger shows some vacillation and less groundedness. In a relationship, look for a long Saturn finger if you are looking for a loyal companion. People with shorter Saturn fingers tend to have less balance and therefore are less likely to stick around for the long haul.

In some hands, the Saturn finger is underdeveloped and is no longer than its neighbors. If one of your other fingers challenges your Saturn finger in height, that finger will also dominate your way of viewing the world. A person with an underdeveloped Saturn finger is likely to feel lacking in harmony. You are apt to be prone to moodiness and depression—you feel lacking of an inner core of strength to anchor you against life's storms.

Curved Saturn finger

Examine both hands to see if either of your middle fingers is curved or leaning toward one of its neighbors. If so, which finger is it leaning toward?

_____

_____

A curved Saturn finger is an indication that the finger toward which it is leaning is exerting undue influence. If Saturn leans toward Jupiter, it a somewhat dangerous sign as it indicates that you may surrender your moral values to your ego and wish for personal power. This was shown to be present on a print of Hitler's fingers. A pronounced leaning Saturn finger should act as a red flag that you may consider yourself to be above the law and will do whatever needs to be done to get your way without worrying about who is hurt in the process.

If the Saturn finger leans toward Apollo, it shows that the artistic and spiritual reign in your life. This may make you somewhat out of touch with the down-to-earth, practical side of life. This tendency has been seen in strong religious figures, including cult leaders. It also may be seen in "starving artists" who sometimes sacrifice their family's welfare for their art.

It is always best for Saturn to be the longest and the straightest finger of your hand. Anything else indicates imbalance. If Saturn is leaning or very short, you should check your non-dominant hand also. If the leaning only occurs in your dominant hand, it is a sign that this imbalance has been caused by societal or familial influences. For example, Saturn leaning toward Apollo could symbolize religious fanaticism. If this is not the case in the non-dominant hand, it is an indicator of imposed beliefs from outside forces. This also means that this trait can be changed if you wish to change. If the leaning is present on both hands, it may be your natural inclination, or even your destiny, to be so inclined and is much less likely to be changed.

Mount of Saturn

Look carefully at the fleshy part of the hand under your Saturn finger. Is it flat, well-developed, or bulbous?

The Mount of Saturn shows the person's conscience. An overdeveloped mount indicates a person with a rigid set of life rules. You tend to be an all-or-nothing sort of person with a very dogmatic point of view. On the other hand, a flat or concave mount indicates that the person plays life as if there are no rules. You are a person with an under-developed conscience who may take advantage of others if given the opportunity to do so.

The best size of mount is a well-developed one which is approximately the same size as the mounts under the other fingers. When comparing mounts, you should look to the other mounts on your hand rather than someone else's. Some people have naturally fleshier hands and larger mounts. To be of consequence, the mounts must be very obviously under or overdeveloped in order for these characteristics to be true.

What have you learned about yourself from examining your Saturn finger?

balanced ~ morally grounded

Is your Saturn finger over or underdeveloped? If so, what does this say about you?

Is your Saturn finger curved? If so, toward which finger? What does this mean?

Straight - balanced

Describe the mount under your Saturn finger? What does it tell you?

indicates conscience - has set of rules but not dogmatic/rigid

Have you learned anything new about the balance in your life, your influence on others, or your value system?

6

Apollo Finger

*T**he Apollo finger symbolizes your spiritual and creative nature.*

Length

An average Apollo finger will reach the middle of the top Saturn phalange. A well-developed Apollo finger is generally considered to be a good sign. It means that you are intuitive and have a balanced spiritual and creative side to your personality. You love beauty and music in all of its forms and have a strong creative urge. When your Apollo finger is straight and fairly long, you have respected this side of your character and honored your creative and spiritual nature. You are in touch with your muse and comfortable with your spirit.

An Apollo finger that is appreciably shorter than average indicates that your character has an underdeveloped side. People with very short Apollo fingers have little or no appreciation for nature or beauty. You have no appreciation for the spiritual, whether in nature, religion, myth, or psyche. You often feel lifeless and "dried up." It is as if something is missing from your life—which is true. You need to develop and cultivate the spirit that is present in us all. While you may not have the capacity to become a psychic or an artist, you do have the possibility to open yourself to nature and its wonders.

An overdeveloped Apollo finger indicates that its owner has a tendency toward boastful behavior. You often have very strong opinions which you seldom keep to yourself. You are often artists or muses who are extreme in your style and taste.

People with very long Apollo fingers are very seductive and flamboyant. You are also very creative and have a strong spiritual nature. You have a great deal of personal magnetism, but also have a tendency toward bravado and exaggeration. You make excellent actors and salespeople. You are not, however, particularly easy to live or work with as you demand the center stage and make unreasonable demands in the name of your "art."

Curved Apollo finger
When the Apollo finger leans toward Saturn it is a sign that the individual's creative and spiritual side is not being nurtured. Crooked fingers always represent a balance problem, unless of course, there is a history of broken bones, arthritis, or other medical explanations.

Crooked fingers typically represent a balance problem.

If the Apollo finger bends toward Mercury, it indicates that the creative side of the person is expressed through the art of verbal expression. You are probably a great storyteller with a touch of the blarney. This is a rare finger sign, and others may be somewhat careful around you as you are not always what you appear to be.

Mount of Apollo
The Mount of Apollo expresses the creative energy of the person. A large Mount of Apollo shows that you possess

energy of expression and are magnetic and charming. You can make style and color work for you, but you can also be a snob about taste.

A weak Mount of Apollo indicates an imitative style of art with little originality. You may appreciate the arts but are unlikely to be an artist. You may, however, excel at various crafts and handwork.

Write here what you have discovered about your spiritual and creative side.

Is your Apollo finger shorter or longer than usual? What does this mean?

_____

_____

_____

Do you have a strong or weak Mount of Apollo? What does this say about you?

_____

_____

_____

_____

...you will get it.
—Jerry Gillies

Is your Apollo finger curved? Towards which finger?

_____

_____

_____

What has looking at your Apollo finger told you about yourself?

_____

_____

_____

_____

_____

7

Mercury Finger

*T*he *finger of Mercury (your little finger) shows*
the amount of life energy you possess and is an
indicator of your sexual magnetism and your
communication skills.

Length

An average Mercury finger should come to the bottom of
the top phalange of Apollo. A well-developed finger of
Mercury indicates someone with good communication
skills and is often found on the hands of attorneys, business
people and salespeople. You have sufficient energy to
handle the demands of difficult jobs with long hours and
still have interest in social and sexual matters.

If your Mercury finger reaches well over the line of the top
phalange of Apollo, your communication skills may be
overdeveloped as well. This finger is seen in the highly
animated speaker who has a tendency to be constantly in
motion. You are the life of the party and make an excellent
salesperson. You do, however, tend to exaggerate for the
sake of a good story or to consummate a sale. A long
Mercury finger is seen on con artists and swindlers, as well
as the super salesperson. Although blessed with abundant
energy, you may neglect other areas of your life for your
career, and you may be overly obsessed with monetary
matters. In relationships, a person with a long Mercury

finger is hard to keep up with and, due to an over-abundance of energy, has a tendency toward unfaithfulness.

The Mercury finger can be shorter than average in two possible ways. If your Mercury finger starts at roughly the same level as the other fingers but is appreciably shorter than the bottom of the top phalange of the Apollo finger, it is considered to be underdeveloped. An underdeveloped Mercury finger indicates that you have communication difficulties. You are prone to stage fright and are fearful of public speaking. You will often appear ill at ease in large groups. People with short little fingers are secretive and are masters of the understatement. You have learned that not revealing all can be very effective.

Another way in which your Mercury finger can be per-ceived as shorter than average is when it starts considerably below the level of the other fingers. In this case your finger itself is not too short, but rather its position is low-set on the hand. A low-set Mercury finger is a sign of a difficult childhood and often is possessed by persons with some degree of immaturity. However, people with a low-set Mercury finger have a delightful childlike character which survives after addressing the trauma of their childhood.

While a low-set finger is a sign of low self-esteem, it also can indicate someone who is a late bloomer. Often you will come into your own in your middle age when you over-come the self-esteem problem which comes from having a dysfunctional family or other childhood difficulties. A low-set Mercury finger is almost always an indicator of childhood problems such as a family history of alcoholism, abuse, or mental illness. This does not mean that you must keep this pattern. While your finger will always remain low-set (in contrast with lines and crooked fingers which will change when you change), you can overcome this problem and be better for it. The key is recognizing yourself and learning the lessons written on your palm.

If your Mercury finger is low-set on your dominant hand, look at the length of the Mercury finger on the non-dominant hand also. If you had a difficult childhood, this finger will be longer. This is a sign that your natural inclination is to be confident and self-assured and that you can be that again.

Curved Mercury finger
In addition to communication, Mercury reveals much about a person's sexual nature. Of course, communication is a large key to a successful sex life. If your little finger curves toward Apollo, you tend to be secretive and contemplative. Others will have to work very hard to learn all of your true nature—unless, of course, they know how to read palms.

If your little finger leans away from Apollo, you are somewhat of a rebel and do not follow the crowd. You will not easily be swayed by opinion.

Mount of Mercury
A well-developed Mount of Mercury indicates that the person is comfortable with public speaking and has good oratorical skill. If the mount is over-developed, the person may not know when to quit talking. If you have ever been in the presence of a "long-winded" orator, you will know what I mean. This person needs to learn moderation in speech and should cultivate the art of listening.

A flat Mount of Mercury belongs to those to whom communication is a problem. You may have difficulties in romantic and sexual relationships as you have trouble putting your feelings into words. A relationship with a person with a very flat or concave Mount of Mercury will feel somewhat lifeless and unexciting since the language of love adds a great deal to the total experience. If you can learn to master some speaking skills, your love life will probably improve also. If this happens, your Mount of Mercury will "perk up" with the rest of your life.

Take some time to analyze what you have learned from your Mercury finger.

What is the length of your Mercury finger? What does this mean?

_____

_____

_____

If your Mercury finger is short, is it low-set or under-developed? If you have a low-set finger, what does this tell you about your childhood and self-esteem? Is this true for you?

_____

_____

_____

Is your Mercury finger curved? What does this say?

_____

_____

_____

Do you have an over or underdeveloped mount? Does
the description seem true to you?

_____

_____

_____

_____

_____

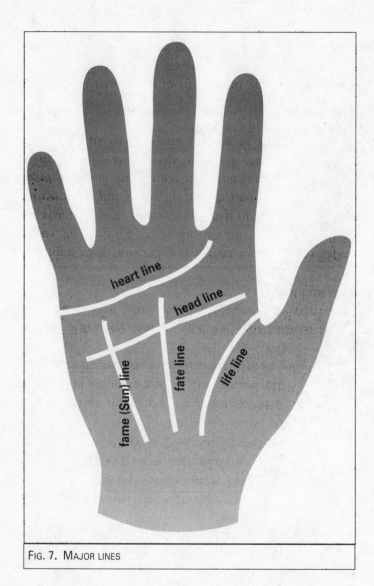

FIG. 7. MAJOR LINES

8

Introduction to Palm Lines

*W*hen *most people think of palmistry, they think of the reading of the lines in the palm. As we have already seen, there is a great deal more to hand analysis than that. However, the lines in your palm do tell many intriguing and useful things about you.*

One of the most interesting and useful things about reading your lines is that they are extremely changeable. Once you have learned a few crucial items, you can monitor your stress level and emotional well-being merely by glancing at the palm of your hand.

It should not be surprising that stress shows itself so quickly on your palm. Every woman knows how quickly stress reveals itself on her face. Your palm is even more vulnerable to the rigors of life. There are innumerable nerve endings in your palm, each of which controls certain features. Once you become familiar with what to look for, you will be surprised that you have not before noticed the day-to-day variations that occur on your palm.

You have probably heard of the three major lines in the palm—the life, heart and head lines. An understanding of these lines is crucial to fully understanding yourself. In addition, there are a number of other small lines which contribute to the full story that your palm has to tell.

The three major lines are a key to your basic personality and, because of this, they change less rapidly than the minor lines in your hand. It is important to read the lines in both hands, if for no other reason than to become aware of the great differences in your hands. Your dominant hand will show the person that you have become because of all of life's various influences. It is also more likely to show major events that have happened in your life. Your non-dominant hand is the hand that will show your potential. It changes far less rapidly than your dominant hand and therefore can give you a clue as to the person you could have been. Look to your non-dominant hand to tell the story of your genetic influences, your inborn character traits, perhaps even your karmic history. A comparison of your two hands shows a clear snapshot of the person you have become—and the person you might have been. Read together, you are given the gift of determining who you wish to be in your future.

A comparison of your two hands shows a clear snapshot of the person you have become–and the person you might have been.

Remember, the purpose of hand analysis is to get to know yourself. In my opinion, our only real task in life is to fully become who we already are.

We will be examining many things about each one of the major lines. The character and quality of the lines is important. You will need to determine whether your lines are deep or shallow, wide or narrow. You will examine your lines for breaks, forks, islands and other irregularities on their surface.

58

It is also important to determine the shape of a line, for example whether it is straight or curved. You will need to determine the beginning point and the termination point of your line. To keep you from preconceived notions as to your character and history, you will draw each line, charting its quality, shape, beginning and end, prior to learning the meaning of the line.

How to age a line

Because the lines on your palm change as you age and experience life, it is important to be able to approximate the age at which a break or other mark occurs on a line. Aging lines is not an exact science, but it can be very useful in determining when certain happenings have occurred. This is also the place where prognostication has value. There are certain markers that seem to have predictive meaning on the lines. It is important to note here that these are just predictions and that, if you change, these predictive marks also will change. This is what I mean when I say that your fortune is not prescribed. The predictive marks on your lines are merely stating that a certain type of event may occur if nothing happens that causes you to change.

You should use these predictive marks as goals and as warnings. If you don't like the prediction, then you must do everything in your power to change the events under which it might occur. If you are anxious for a particular happening, then you should structure your life so as to encourage and nurture that event.

The head and life lines are read from the inside of the palm (near the thumb) to the outside of the palm. The heart line is read in just the opposite way, from the outside (little finger side) to the inside. This means, for example, that breaks, marks, or meshing near the thumb on your life line are indicative of happenings in your early childhood and adolescent years. On your heart line, the early marks would show nearest the little finger side of the line.

To determine the approximate time of your life when certain happenings may occur along your various lines, you mentally divide each line into seven sections, each approximating a ten year period of time. This is, of course, assuming many things which may not come true, such as living to the age of seventy. Nonetheless, a seventy-year life span is an average life span and is therefore used for aging. If you are expecting an exact date, you are going to be quite disappointed. The best you should hope for is an approximate time of life, such as childhood, mid-life, or old age.

Fig. 8 shows a palm on which the major lines have been aged. You can use this as an example of how to age your palm, remembering that these ages are just approximations, not exact dates.

Minor or temporary marks
After you have *aged* your lines, you can better determine when a certain event may happen or when it occurred. Each break, island, square or netting can be read as an occurrence on the lines. Remember, though, that the heart line is read from the outside in, and that the life and head lines are read from the opposite direction.

The various marks found along your three major lines must be interpreted within the context of that line's total meaning. These marks may appear and disappear depending upon where you are in your life. Here are some general rules for interpreting the marks on your major lines. These

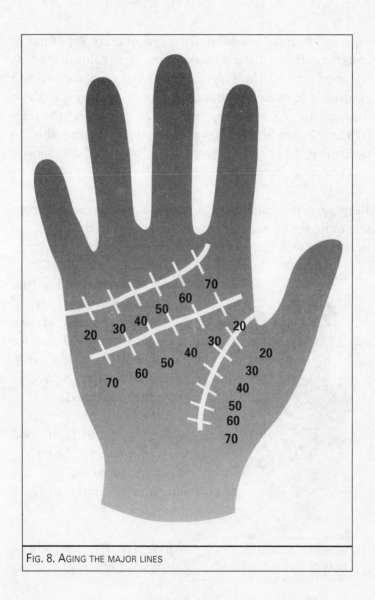

FIG. 8. AGING THE MAJOR LINES

must be interpreted carefully. If a meaning does not make sense to you in the context of the line or in your memory of your life, then you should disregard it. Not all marks have meaning and not all meaning is known.

Figs. 9, 10, and 11 show illustrations of examples of minor markings. If you have a marking on your palm or on one of your major lines, you should try to define the approximate shape of the marking by comparing it to these illustrations. Your marking will not be exactly like the ones in the illustrations. However, you should be able to determine the shape of the marking by use of comparison and common sense.

Keeping that in mind, the general rule is that *squares* on a line indicate that some factor of that line is in the process of being repaired or corrected.

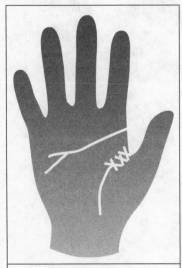

FIG. 9. BRANCH ON HEAD LINE, MESH OR NETTING ON LIFE LINE

Mesh or netting on a line occurs at a time of stress. Netting or mesh at the beginning of the life line, for example, is a sign of a stressful and perhaps abusive or traumatic childhood.

Crosses can mean both good or bad fortune, but they usually occur at the time of a memorable happening in your life.

Stars usually mean the fulfillment of dreams. They

are often seen on the head and heart lines.

Islands on a line point to periods of weakness and blocked energy in your life. The nature of the weakness is read according to the meaning of the line. If you see islands in your hand dating from this current time of your life, you should be very careful not to overstress or tax yourself.

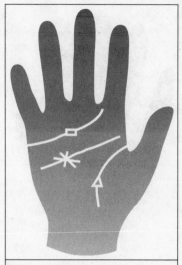

FIG. 10. SQUARE, STAR, TRIANGLE

Triangles are a good sign, and usually highlight a happy event.

If your hand has a great deal of netting or meshing outside the major lines, it is a sure sign that you are under stress. The more minor markings of this sort, the higher will be the stress level.

Finally, *breaks* mean just that. They are a sign of an ending, perhaps of a relationship or a career, perhaps of a dream or an interest. If the broken line begins again in a new direction, it means a complete change.

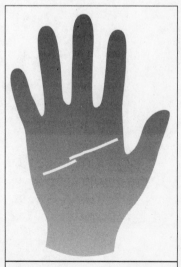

FIG. 11. BREAK ON HEAD LINE

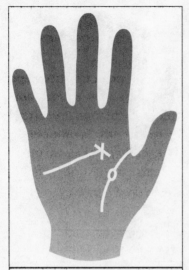

FIG. 12. CROSS ON HEAD LINE,
ISLAND ON LIFE LINE

Because these marks can be difficult to read, you must ask yourself "What is this mark saying to me about this area of my life?" This is where your intuition and psychic ability must come into play. Never let someone give you an interpretation that doesn't feel correct to you. This is your palm and your life. You are the final decision-maker as to your destiny. Never give away your power in this regard. Watch your hands and chart your path.

9

Heart Line

*T**he heart line provides you with information about
your emotional strength and well-being, your
approach to love interests and, to a certain extent, the
line gives a history of your life's loves and heartbreaks.*

It is the upper-most major line on your palm, starting slightly
below your little finger and running across your palm,
generally ending between your Jupiter and Saturn fingers.

Learning to read this line will provide you with valuable
insight into your method of dealing with emotional
subjects and feelings.

Contrary to the other two major lines on your palm, the
heart line is read from the Mercury finger over to the
Jupiter finger. You can date occurrences on your heart line
similar to the way you do on all other lines. Emotional
heartbreak will be reflected on your heart line as a break.
Breaks in your heart line may also mean other forms of
emotional trauma as well as the end of an affair or a
significant illness.

Small lines branching upward from your heart line indicate
happy and pleasant occurrences, such as pleasant love affairs
and good friendships. Small lines branching downward can

be read as affairs or relationships which ended on an unhappy or luckless note and caused some sadness or heartbreak.

In the palm below sketch your heart line as you see it on your dominant hand. Make sure to draw it as it is on your palm including the approximate angle of the line and the correct ending place, for example under the Jupiter finger, between the Jupiter and Saturn fingers etc. If you see any breaks or branches sketch them in also.

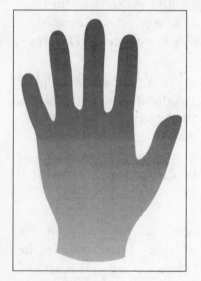

After you have sketched this line as correctly as possible, take a minute to examine the quality of your heart line. Use of a magnifying glass may help you to see all the breaks, islands and other markings on the line. Now make a few notes in the space provided about what you have observed.

Are there any major breaks on your heart line?

_____

If so, approximately at what time in your life did they occur? (See aging your line for help.)

....

Are there any islands, stars, triangles, netting or other marks on your heart line?

_____

If so, what are they, and at what age do they occur?

_____

_____

After you have completed your analysis, read on for the interpretation of your line.

Shape of the heart line

Perhaps the most important feature of the heart line is the differentiation between straight and curved heart lines.

Fig. 13 shows examples of curved and straight heart lines. Your line may fall anywhere in between these two examples.

Curved heart line

If your heart line curves up, you fall in love impulsively, show your feelings openly, and wear your heart on your sleeve. You are easily hurt in love, but you also bounce back quickly from a broken heart. You have a lot of emotional energy and are very sensitive. You thrive on passion and romance and may become disappointed if you enter a relationship where the other person doesn't view and express love in the same flamboyant manner that you do. The depth of your craving for romance will be reflected in the slope of your curve. It is not a measurement of your ability to love, but your method of showing that love.

A drastic curve is the sign of a great romantic. You expect constant attention and flowers and need to hear the words "I love you" on a daily basis. A more slowly-pitched curve is still a mark of a demonstrative person, but you are less demanding of outward attention. You give a lot of nurture, hugs and support to everyone around you. You are apt to

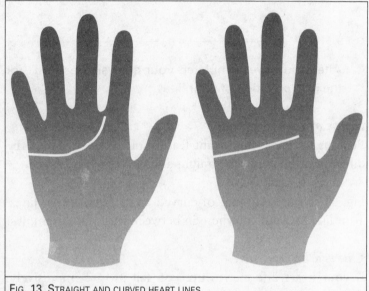

FIG. 13. STRAIGHT AND CURVED HEART LINES

make a less demonstrative, less showy person rather nervous. You just won't know what a curved-heart-line person is apt to do.

If your heart line is straight or has a very small curve, you are much more apt to think before you fall in love. You are less demonstrative and less likely to show your feelings. You are no less loving and are perhaps more steady in your loyalty. Straight-heart-line people make great spouses and

68

lovers but may be unable to fully show the depth of their devotion. The shorter your straight heart line is, the more rational is likely to be your approach to love. You must be careful, if you have a short straight heart line, that you do not think yourself completely out of a relationship. Short-straight-heart-line people tend to be somewhat dominant and self-controlled. You may need to make extra efforts to demonstrate your love to your spouse or significant other who may not completely understand or appreciate your rational approach to love.

Long, straight heart lines belong to very intense people who bring great energy to their relationships. You can be very possessive and have a tendency toward unreasonable jealousy. You are loyal and protective and expect the same in return. You love with 100 percent of yourself. Your love may feel overwhelming to someone who loves with a lighter approach.

The depth of your craving for romance will be reflected in the slope of your curve.

A line that turns down at the end toward the head line is found in people who tend toward being cold-natured, moody, and difficult. This is a somewhat rare curve as most heart lines curve up rather than down. If you are in a relationship with a person whose heart line turns down, you can expect that this relationship will not be easy. Although capable of great love, the person may also be quite a trial to live with. If you have such a line, you may wish to lighten up on your approach to love and life. It will help to change your world view to a less pessimistic and gloomy model. If you do, you may find that the curve on your heart line will begin to turn up as you change your perpetual frown into a smile.

If your heart line turns downward and actually joins the head line, it suggests a tendency to be violent. If it then joins with the life line, there is a possibility of a violent streak toward self or family. I would be hesitant to become romantically involved with the possessor of such a line. If your line reflects these tendencies, search your character for signs of rage and violence. All character traits can be changed, and self-knowledge is the key to starting this change. If violence is part of your life, there are ways to eliminate it. Embrace peace and your heart line will begin to take an upward climb.

Physical Signs

Reading the heart line can also give some indication of your physical strength and vulnerabilities. Needless to say, this is an inexact measurement at best and certainly should not be relied upon to the exclusion of medical treatment or advice. However, doctors themselves will often look at the color and condition of hands and fingers for signs of physical difficulties.

A double heart line is a sign of great physical strength. Sometimes called the "sister line," an extra heart line "doubles" the quality of the line. In addition to great physical strength, people with double heart lines often have great emotional strength as well. In a straight-heart-line person, a doubled line would indicate immense emotional control. It would be very hard for others to get to know you as you would control your emotions with an iron will. In a curved-heart-line person, you would find someone in love with the world. Highly demonstrative, this person would literally overwhelm you with his or her emotional strength and character.

In very rare cases, the heart and head lines run together as one line. In traditional palmistry this is called the Simian line. It indicates that the ability to reason and the ability to feel do not function separately from one another. This marker is often found in the hands of those with Down's Syndrome, but certainly is not an indicator of that condition.

Take a few minutes to analyze what you have learned from your heart line.

What does the shape of your heart line tell you about your approach to love and relationships?

_____

_____

_____

_____

What do the breaks and markings on your heart line say to you?

_____

_____

_____

_____

Did you learn anything about your physical strength or vulnerability?

_____

_____

_____

Does this seem correct to you? In what way?

_____

_____

_____

_____

_____

_____

10

Head Line

*T*he head line lies directly below the heart line and
above the life line. It illustrates your mode of
*thinking, your ability to rationalize, and your
approach to life.*

Contrary to public opinion, the head line does not tell how
intelligent you are. Rather it shows your attitudes toward
life, your philosophy, your talents, and your abilities.

You will first want to look at the head line of your dominant hand. This will show you how you think and your
current attitudes toward life. However, you should also
look at your non-dominant head line. If the head lines on
your two hands are very different, it is a sign that you have
talents and ambitions that have not been realized.

The head line is read from the Jupiter finger across the palm,
and can be aged by the method we have discussed earlier.

On the hand illustrated below, sketch your head line,
paying careful attention to the slope of the line. Look
carefully at whether your head line touches your life
line, and if it does, sketch in that intersection also.
Finally, add any breaks or branches that may occur on
your head line.

After you have sketched your head line, take a moment to examine it carefully and answer the following questions.

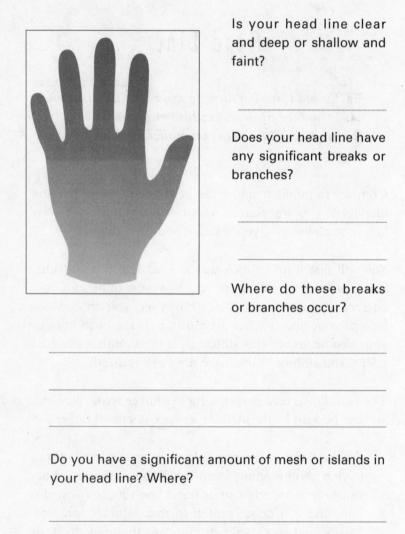

Is your head line clear and deep or shallow and faint?

_____

Does your head line have any significant breaks or branches?

_____

_____

Where do these breaks or branches occur?

_____

_____

_____

Do you have a significant amount of mesh or islands in your head line? Where?

_____

_____

Does your head line intersect with your life line?

_____

If so, is there a significant amount of netting at that intersection?

_____

If your head line does not intersect with your life line, how large is the gap between the beginnings of both lines? Measure this gap with a ruler.

_____

Does your head line terminate in a straight line, fork, or branch?

_____

Now that you have finished with this analysis, here is what your head line is telling you.

Quality of the head line
The deeper and clearer the line, the stronger the thinking process. Deep head lines belong to those who are confident and dynamic. Shallow lines are a sign of one who is intuitive and sensitive but less clear and confident in their thinking.

Islands and meshing are signs of nervousness and anxiety. Like minor lines, these marks will come and go in a person's life. If you have a great deal of meshing or netting, you are probably susceptible to insomnia and worry. You may be under a great deal of stress. This is an extremely common symptom of our society. Monitoring the meshing and stress lines on your head line can give you insight into the effect stress has on your physical body. Often we are so used to the amount of pressure in our lives that we are not consciously aware of it. You can be sure, however, that if this stress is appearing on your head line, it is also affecting other areas of your body. By reading the stress on your head line, you can perhaps head off other stress-related symptoms that take longer to develop, such as high blood pressure, heart difficulties, sleep disorders, and the myriad other physical signs supplied by our bodies when we refuse to acknowledge stress in our lives.

Ideally, both logic and imagination are available to every person. Using one to the exclusion of the other means a lack of balance in your life.

By aging your line, you should be able to approximate the time when stress and difficulty occur. Islands indicate blockages of some type. If you have an island on your head line at the current time, you have an issue that needs to be resolved in your life.

Shape of the head line

The shape and pitch of the head line will tell you if your primary way of thinking is by logic or intuition.

If your head line is straight, your method of thinking will be one of realism with logic and reason prevailing in your life. You have a good memory, and you reason your way through life by weighing your past experiences and learning from the present situation. You have good powers of concentration and strong will power. If you aren't careful, however, you may be perceived by others as cold and calculating or unfeeling.

A curved head line is a sign of a creative thinker whose imagination governs your thoughts. You see possibilities and act on them. You are bold and inventive, but dealing with you can be frustrating to a straight-head-line person who can't see your logic or plan of attack.

Curved-head-line people belong in the creative fields such as marketing and advertising. You are capable of planning, but you don't always carry out that plan. You are not always realistic, and you have a tendency to overspend on a project. You also tend to exaggerate and can experience severe mood swings.

If your head line takes a deep dip, you are a dreamer who may also be overly sensitive. You are prone to never completing a project because you are already dreaming of the next one. Just as with the heart line, the pitch of the curve dictates the intensity of characteristics. A deeply curved head line is indicative of imagination reigning in your life.

Ideally, both logic and imagination are available to every person. Using one to the exclusion of the other means a lack of balance in your life.

Termination of the head line

How a line terminates tells you a great deal about your character. A solid ending is usually found in a person with a single point of view. You believe strongly that your way is the right way.

Forked endings are sometimes called writer's or lawyer's forks. These are people who can see both sides to the story and both points of view. However, a fork at the end of the head line can also tell you that you are facing a decision or

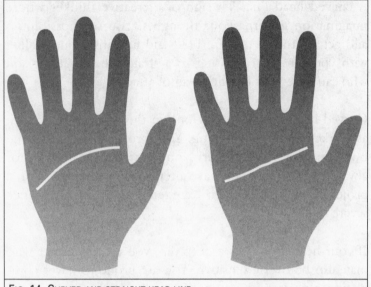

FIG. 14. CURVED AND STRAIGHT HEAD LINE

heading for a change. If you have many forks at the end of various lines on your palm, you are probably at a time of transition in your life.

Large branches at the end of your head line can indicate two different personalities between which you may vacillate from day to day. This is exciting for some but it can be rather frustrating and unnerving to those who have to deal with you on a day-to-day basis.

If your head line ends in a three-pronged fork, you see things in an unusual fashion. You are considered somewhat bizarre in your way of viewing the world. This trait can make you both peculiar and intriguing. It is a rare mark, but one seen in the hand of visionaries and seers.

Branches

Branches occurring along the head line are markers of events in your life. When the branches head downward, they are telling of a time in your life when you were suffering from worry and mental strain. These times may have been accompanied by severe depression. If the branch downward is under a particular finger, then that finger's traits were the subject of your depression. For example, a branch under your Jupiter finger symbolizes depression and worry in regard to your ambition and leadership. If the branch occurs under your Saturn finger, it could symbolize a religious or value worry. Branching under Mercury often tells of sexual concerns or communication problems. As these branches are "aged," the approximate time of the stress can then be ascertained.

Branches upward show just the opposite. They are indicators of optimism that materialize toward the subject matter of the finger to which the branches are pointed.

You will develop an upward branch on your head line during times of great excitement and anticipation. These branches do not necessarily indicate great occurrences in your life. Rather, they show your mental state in anticipating or relishing these happenings. Just as in downward branches, the subject of this excitement is related to the finger at which the branch aims. An upward branch toward Jupiter tells of the dreams of the extrovert. It is a time for drama, leadership and ambition. If the branch aims for Saturn, it indicates a yearning for strong religious convictions or moral values. Branches toward Apollo indicate interests in creative and spiritual endeavors. Upward branches reaching for Mercury show high excitement in the sexual and relationship areas.

Life line merger

Perhaps one of the most important things to look for when examining your head line is whether or not it merges at its source with the life line. To the extent that the head and life line merge, it symbolizes the effect which your family of origin, and society in general, have on you. When your head line and life line do not touch, you are an independent thinker who may be a bit of a rebel. You did not allow your family's values and ways of thinking to highly influence you. You have your own values and beliefs and only are influenced by other people if you believe they are correct.

The wider the gap between these two lines, the more independent you are. People with a large gap, one-half centimeter or more, may be overly rash, insensitive, and rebellious. You would not be a particularly good employee, although you do very well working for yourself. In a relationship, you need to make your own way and be coupled with someone equally as independent. You are not afraid to break the rules; as a matter of fact, you don't think the rules apply to you.

> To the extent that the head and life line merge, it symbolizes the effect which your family of origin, and society in general, have on you.

People whose head line merges with their life line are much more likely to worry about other people's perceptions and opinions. You make good employees and responsible spouses. However, if this merger continues for a centimeter or more, you may still be enmeshed with your family of origin. You were highly influenced by your parents and may still be caught up in parental expectations and family mores.

If your head line is merged with your life line for a distance, it is likely that you are still dealing with parental issues. I often see this meshing in hands of those who are dealing with painful issues of parental aging, or who are just now facing issues of childhood dysfunction or abuse. By aging your life line, you can see at what time you are able to escape this enmeshment. People who are currently caught up in family-of-origin issues will have a great deal of netting and islands along the early part of their life-head intersection. It may even be a darker or redder color than the rest of the line.

Meshing, netting or other signs of stress at the beginning of your life-head line merger are a clear sign of trouble in childhood. Meshing and islands at the beginning of your life line, whether or not the life line merges with the head line, are a sign of childhood illness, trauma or dysfunction in the family.

The further the meshing or netting occurs on your life line, the more likely it is that you are still affected by difficulties of some sort with your family of origin. When the meshing continues for a long time on your head line too, it means that your thoughts and behavior are still highly affected by childhood family patterns and influences. Even if your parents are deceased, you may still be playing out some old family drama. Therapy or self-introspection can help you break out of this mode. In a few months or years, you may examine your hands and be surprised to see that a good deal of meshing and netting has disappeared.

Length
The longer your head line, the more abstract your thinking will be. People whose head lines cover the entire length of

their palm are the eggheads of society. You agonize over problems, weighing the pros and cons before making your decision. You see shades of gray where your short-head-line neighbors see only black and white.

A short line shows that its possessor has good common sense but does not think in abstract ways. The shorter the line, the more instinctual the thinking. A short head line means that you act with a high degree of impulsiveness. This does not have to do with your amount of intellect, but rather your method of thinking. As a short-head-line person you probably arrive at a solution to a problem considerably faster than a long-head-line friend. However, since you have not weighed all the alternatives, that solution could be disastrous.

Now that you have completed your analysis of your head line, write a synopsis here of your way of thinking, analyzing and viewing life.

Is your head line straight or curved? What does this mean about your way of thinking?

_____

_____

How does your head line terminate? What does this mean?

_____

Do you have any branches from your head line? If so, what does this say to you?

_____

_____

Does your head line merge at its origin with your life line? If so, how long do they run together? What does this mean to you?

_____

_____

_____

If your head line does not merge with your life line, what does this say about you?

_____

_____

_____

Do you have netting, meshing or islands at the beginning of your life-head line merger? What does this mean? Does this seem accurate to you?

_____

_____

How long is your head line? What does this mean?

_____

_____

_____

Does this analysis seem correct to you? Why or why not?

_____

_____

_____

_____

_____

11

Life Line

Your life line represents your life force and your vitality. It starts on the inside edge of your palm above your thumb and sweeps to the base of your palm.

The life line has little if anything to do with your life span, but it does give clues into your physical health. Do not be overly concerned, therefore, if you possess a short life line. Your life line will grow and change as you grow and change. As a child, my life line was extremely short and faint, barely taking me to the age of thirty. At the age of thirty I was hospitalized with a life-threatening illness and spent six weeks in the Intensive Care Unit. Although I was very sick, I did survive, and now, twelve years later, my life line has grown to show a long life. It does, however, reflect the trauma of my illness by a sharp break at approximately age thirty. It also shows signs of physical trauma and weakness.

> The life line has little if anything to do with your life span...Your life line will grow and change as you grow and change.

If you learn to read your life line, you also will be able to watch your life experiences become reflected upon it. You will learn to look for interruptions in the line indicating illness, trauma, or change. You will also learn to look to the quality and length of the line for signs of vitality.

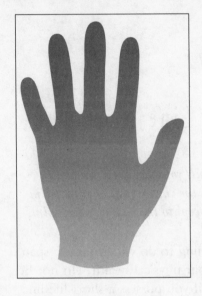

On the illustration at left, chart the path of your life line. Draw it as accurately as you can, paying attention to its length and path. Also draw in any breaks, islands or meshing that occur along the line.

Now that you have sketched your life line, analyze it carefully and answer the following questions.

Is your life line deep or faint?

_____

Do you see any sign of meshing, islands or breaks? Describe these markings and indicate their approximate location by the aging method.

_____

_____

Do these breaks head for a particular finger? If so, which one?

_____

_____

What is the pitch of your life line? Does it cross your palm or hug closely to your thumb?

Depth of the line

Very deep life lines are an indication of high physical energy and vigor. People with this type of line are often described as having boundless energy. You can be very demanding to those around you, as you often don't have patience for those of us with a higher need for rest and calm. You don't always understand or sympathize with physically weaker people, and you often run other people ragged. Working or living with you can be exhausting. However, you are a person who will give that "110 percent" athletes often talk about. Those who can stand to be around this bundle of energy will be in the presence of a highly productive person.

The average life line is deep but not a ravine—it belongs to people with sufficient energy to handle life's demands, but also people who need sleep, rest, and vacations.

A shallow, light life line is a sign of people who have low physical energy but are highly sensitive to others and to conditions around them. This sensitivity can cause you to be exhausted when overwhelmed by others or events. You need more than an average time of sleep, rest, vacations, and solitude. You are likely to feel drained by the psychic energy of others. You are not good when combined with very high-energy people. You make excellent social workers, ministers, and nurses, but you are prone to illness if you don't take care of yourself.

Breaks in the life line

Breaks in your life line most often symbolize problems, uncertainties, illnesses, or accidents. If the line breaks completely and then starts up in another direction, it is a clear sign that you have overcome the difficulty and have headed toward your goal again, but perhaps on a slightly different path.

A sudden break in a life line that then starts up again somewhere else, indicates that you will have a dramatic change in your life which will completely change your way of life and viewpoint. Some people have many breaks in their life line symbolizing many dramatic life-style changes. A person with drastic changes in the past is probably going to have more in the future.

If your life line breaks and starts again closer to the Mount of Venus, near the thumb, you have made a dramatic choice of a quieter, more spiritual life style. This is the sign of one who has moved from the city to the country, changed from a big law firm to self-employment, or joined a spiritual community. If it happens toward the end of the life line, it indicates retirement to a quieter community or lifestyle.

As you read the breaks in your life line, you may be amazed at how often they accurately describe times of problems and illnesses in your life. Breaks that appear to occur in the future have a predictive quality about them. Remember that the future is not carved in stone. If you can determine what the cause of the break may be, perhaps you can prevent the difficulty from occurring. I have seen hands in which the life line has changed dramatically after the person changed equally as dramatically. A divorce, recovery from addiction, or a change in career will have an effect, either positive or negative, on your life line.

Branches

The breaks, branches, and marks on your life line tell the stories of your life. Branches from the life line going up denote achievement and rewards. Lines that shoot up toward the fingers indicate efforts toward a goal. You can pinpoint the type of goal by looking toward which finger a line is pointing. If the branch points to your Jupiter finger, your primary goal is for power and ambitious striving. If it points to Saturn, your goal is for balance and stability. Branches aiming toward Apollo show achievement in arts or spiritual realms. Finally, if a branch points to Mercury, the reward is in the field of communications.

Lines branching downward on your life line reflect life's less pleasant occurrences. They show your disappointments and broken dreams. Branches are less likely than breaks to reflect physical illnesses and more likely to reflect emotional trauma or heartbreak.

Lines that cross the life line, rather than simply starting at the life line and branching off of it, are called interference lines. When these lines cross the Mount of Venus, the mount under your thumb, it means that others in your life, probably family members, are trying to influence you. The closer these lines are to the beginning of your life line, the more they are likely to indicate parental influence.

Marks

Marks along the life line indicate various happenings which can be aged as discussed earlier. Your life line, more than any other line in your palm, reflects your true life's path.

For this purpose, the dominant hand is the accurate hand to read. The marks on the non-dominant hand will not necessarily show what has happened to you as much as they will show what *could* have happened to you.

Any time you have an island on a line, you are dealing with a situation of blocked energy. These are usually caused by difficult situations where you can't seem to find a way out. Islands indicate a time of high stress and often are accompanied by depression or other activities such as inappropriate use of alcohol, food, or sex as a way to try to break through the trapped feeling.

A fork in your life line shows that a decision has been or will need to be made. A fork at the end of, or branching from, the life line is considered by many palmists to be a travel line and is said to belong to those with wanderlust. I believe this is often true because moving is one possible choice to be made by people who are faced with a life decision. However, the general rule about a fork on your life line is that you are approaching a decision and a possible life change. A geographic change is only one of the many choices you may need to make. A fork on your life line will come and go at times when major life decisions need to be made. I believe that a fork at the end of the life line is a message that you will soon face a choice that will, in some way, change your life. Forks on the other major lines also indicate decisions to be made in conjunction with the meaning of those lines.

Chains on your life line generally indicate physical problems such as minor health disturbances. If you have chains on your life line you are likely to have a history of allergies and other immune system disorders.

A doubled life line is a sign of extreme vitality and is thought to be a symbol of a person who lives a charmed life. This is sometimes called the inner line of life and runs inside the life line close to the thumb. This line gives additional strength and is found in those with strong inner character and spiritual sensitivity. It is quite rare for any major line to be doubled, and therefore this doubling lends extra strength to the line's character.

Curve of the life line

An ideal life line forms almost a perfect circle from the inside of the thumb to the base of the palm. This indicates someone with a longing for a peaceful and serene life. These people usually lead lives of peace and harmony. I do not often see severe breaks, islands, or meshing in these hands. It is also somewhat rare in the hectic and stressful western world in which we live.

When your life line crosses into the middle of your palm, it indicates that you love to travel and often possess an unusual life style. This line is wider than a circle, less curving, and heads for the opposite side of the palm from your thumb. In general, the wider the life line, the more wanderlust you will have, and the less traditional you will be. When your life line cuts completely across your palm, you have an itchy foot and won't be happy in one place or with a standard lifestyle. You tend not to cling to posses-sions as you don't want anything to weigh you down. If you are involved with such people, you will have to keep up

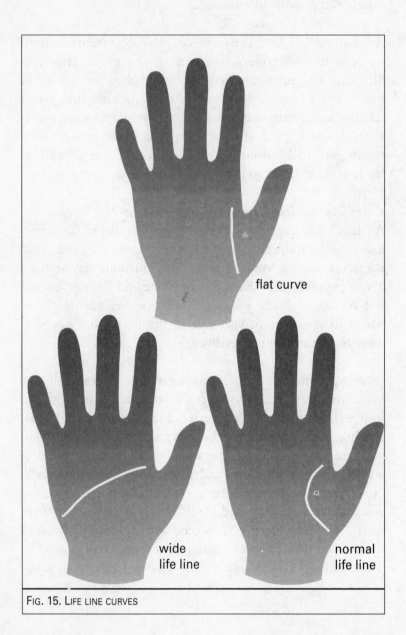

flat curve

wide
life line

normal
life line

Fig. 15. Life line curves

or you might be seen as weighing them down. Also, check the beginning of your life line for interference lines. If there are many interference lines, you could be fleeing early family dysfunctions.

A wide life line that heads toward the base of the palm without much of a curve is a sign of a person with rather simple desires. You also wish to travel but in a plainer fashion and in a less flamboyant manner. You goals tend to be visionary and spiritual. The mystics of the world are likely to bear this line. Material things mean little to you. You are somewhat unpredictable and hard to influence as your values are contrary to the normal values of society.

A line that clings closely to your thumb indicates that you have a careful and cautious approach to life. You wish only to stay close to home where you have deep roots and strong ties. You feel most secure in your house, neighborhood, and home town and are rather traditional in your approach to life. Don't expect someone with a life line that clings to the thumb to be an adventurer. You are dependable and supportive and will chose to remain a homebody if given what you wish.

When your life line curves widely around your thumb, you have a huge appetite for all things. You have a great desire for life's pleasures and for worldly goods. You wish to travel in style and to have a lavish and luxurious home. Your voracious appetite sometimes makes you seem greedy, but this is not actually the case. You simply love the things and the pleasures of the world. Unfortunately, life is not always so generous, and you are often disappointed. You are people who, no matter how much you have, will never quite feel that you have enough.

Now that you have completed your analysis of your life line, write a short synopsis of its meaning.

What does the depth of your life line say about your energy and vigor?

_____

_____

_____

Do you have any breaks in your life line? About when do they occur? What do they mean?

_____

_____

_____

Do you have any branches off your life line? What do they mean?

_____

_____

_____

Are there any marks on your life line? What do they tell you?

_____

_____

_____

What is the curve of your life line? Does this tell you anything about your approach to life?

_____

_____

_____

Do these interpretations seem correct to you? Does this translation fit your understanding of your life to date?

_____

_____

_____

_____

_____

_____

12

Secondary Lines

The major or primary lines of your palm are the heart, head, and life lines. All of the other lines of your hand are considered secondary lines.

The secondary lines of your palm are less caused by genetic and inherent characteristics and more caused by your own determination, will to succeed, and life history. As such, they are far more changeable and tend to come and go and change direction and character on a more regular basis.

The secondary lines do not appear on every hand, and everyone doesn't have every secondary line. As you read this chapter, be aware that you may not be able to find every secondary line on your hand. Do not be disappointed if you do not see a particular line or lines. The line may not be an indicator of your personality, or it may not develop until later in your life when you have experienced more and changed your character in some fashion. These lines can be quite faint and it may help to use a magnifying glass and a bright light in order to search for the secondary lines. If you cannot find a particular line, you should assume that you do not have that line and go on to the next section. In a few months when you re-examine your palms, make sure to look again for these lines—they may have appeared!

In general, the deeper and darker your secondary lines, the more permanent the line and the characteristic. However, remember that these traits vary and change just as you do. Get in the habit of checking your hands on a regular basis. This will give you a clue as to the direction your life is taking, and the areas of importance to you at the current time.

Of the secondary lines, the most important line is the fate line. This line will be discussed in some depth as it gives such a clear view of your career and vocational paths. The next most interesting secondary line is the sun, or fame, line. This line is less common and the information received by this line is less likely to be totally accurate. The sun line is, in some fashion, more of a predictive line than the major lines. Finally, I will discuss some of the other secondary lines, such as the lines of affection, girdle of Venus, and other minor lines that may not appear in every hand.

You should consider these last chapters as an advanced palmistry course. Do not be overly concerned if you cannot find these marks, or if you are confused by their meaning. Understanding the shape of your hand and fingers, and being able to read the three major lines of your hand, will give you much of the information you need to know yourself. The secondary lines are discussed for your enjoyment and to round out your assessment of your character. Take what seems true to you and read the rest for fun.

Fate line
The fate line is also known as the karma or destiny line. It gives you an intriguing look into your life's true work. To read this line, it is crucial that you read the fate lines in both your dominant and non-dominant hand. Your dominant hand's fate line will show your life's path as it has been

shaped by the events of your childhood and the events thus far in your life. The fate line in your non-dominant hand will show your destiny as it was written at the time of your birth. Often these are very different. A well-etched fate line in your dominant hand and not in your other hand is a sign of a self-made person. If you have a well-defined fate line in your non-dominant hand only, that is a sign of unfulfilled potential.

Get in the habit of checking your hands on a regular basis. This will give you a clue as to the direction your life is taking.

The fate line is sometimes called the vocational line, as it gives a sense of purpose to your life and career. It rises from the base of your hand and runs vertically toward your fingers, dividing your hand. The key to understanding your fate line is to understand the characteristics of the various fingers and their mounts—the fate line points to the finger and mount which most accurately reflects your true life's path in regard to your vocational calling.

Fig. 16 shows the approximate location of the fate line. Fate lines can, however, take many shapes and occur at many locations. The darkest and deepest vertical line on your palm is likely to be your fate line.

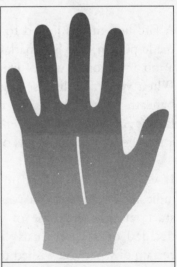

Location of the fate line
If the fate line runs up the middle of your palm toward

FIG. 16. FATE LINE

your Jupiter finger, it indicates that you possess a will to succeed, and is a sign of ambition in your career. This indicates that you have good powers of concentration and determination and would be a good business person. This configuration is also often found in the hands of persons in the legal and law enforcement fields.

When the fate line cuts through the center of your hand, angling toward Saturn, it the sign of a born leader. You would be a good administrator or politician, particularly if your Saturn finger is long and straight.

A fate line that aims toward Apollo predicts a career in the arts fields, such as music, drama, and architecture.

If your fate line points to your Mercury finger, you would do well in a career in which you use the gift of communication. This line is often found in the hands of preachers, broadcasters, and journalists.

A fate line that is joined to the life line is a sign of a self-made person, and is a mark of a person whose career is less a job and more a way of life—you should be self-employed. When your fate line springs from the Mount of Venus, beneath your thumb, your destiny is in the hands of your family. Any successful career will have to take into consideration the wishes and needs of your family.

If your fate line starts in the middle of your palm, it indicates a late start on your life's career. Conversely, if it starts at the very base of your palm, it shows that you decided on a career early in life, and have always been certain of what you wished to be.

Sometimes, the fate line starts low and ends in mid-palm. This means that your career started early and will end early. This is often the sign of a conscious choice to leave the rat race, and is frequently seen in people who plan to or have already retired early.

When your fate line springs from your head line, it predicts a late start on a new career.

If your fate line starts at your heart line, your career is secondary to your love life. No career will be successful for you unless you can incorporate your spouse or lover. Your career may never be the most important part of your life— and you will not want it to be.

Character of the fate line

A deep continuous line shows that the incentive to make a career is strong and is an indication of someone with a great deal of drive and ambition.

If your fate line is frayed or contains islands, you probably lack focus. You may have had many careers, but still feel that you "don't know what you want to do when you grow up."

A line that is over-long, running from the very bottom of the palm to the base of the fingers, is a sure sign of a workaholic.

If your fate line is broken, it indicates that it is time for you to reassess your life. You should look to see if it starts up again on the same path, or if it takes a completely different path. Many times a break in the fate line ushers in a radically new way of looking at one's life. If your line breaks and begins again closer to the outside of your palm, you are likely to develop a deeper appreciation for spiritual and creative goals. Often, this is an indication that you have "loosened up" in your middle years and have slowed down from your career path.

If your fate line breaks and begins again closer to your thumb, it indicates that you have become more disciplined and ambitious. This sign is often seen in the hands of persons recovering from drugs, alcohol, gambling, or other destructive habits.

A fate line that ends in a fork is a sign that you will soon need to make a decision in your life. Forks on the fate line often portend a change of career.

A star at the end of a fate line is a prediction of success. In contrast, islands or breaks along the fate line are indications of difficulties or hard luck.

A few people have no fate line. Contrary to some palmists, this is not an unlucky sign. It indicates that you have no set path before you. This is the hand of the free spirit, a person with no set agenda. This does not mean that you will be unsuccessful, but rather that your career is secondary. You are a person who can be highly successful in a job, only to drop it without a care and head merrily off on a new adventure.

When lines of interference cross your fate line, you are likely to be under a great deal of career stress. If these lines also cross your life line, the stress is coming from concerns about family issues.

If you have a fate line, analyze its meaning at this time.

Do you have a fate line? To which finger does it point?
What does this say to you?

_____

_____

_____

Where does it start? What does this mean?

_____

_____

_____

What are your fate line's characteristics? Is it deep? Are
there markings? Is it broken? What does this tell you?

_____

_____

_____

Do you have lines of interference?

_____

_____

_____

If you have no fate line, what does this mean?

....

_____

....

Does this analysis fit with your view of yourself? Why or why not?

_____

....

_____

Sun (fame) line

This line is also called the Apollo line or the fame line. The sun line is not found in every hand and there is some dispute about its true meaning. Therefore, you should not be disappointed if your hand is missing this line. The line of Sun, (if you have one) runs from the middle of your hand to the vicinity of your Apollo finger. It can, however, point toward the Saturn or Mercury finger as well.

It is easy to confuse the fate line and the fame line. If you only have one line running vertically from the base of the palm to your fingers, it is the fate line and should be read as such. Your fame line would be to the outside of the fate line. It is usually, but not always, a fainter and harder to read line.

Fig. 17 shows the fame line in relation to the fate line. Like the fate line, the fame line can be hard to find. If you have two vertical lines on your hand, the fainter line is likely to be the fame line.

The sun line is a sign of artistic or creative talent and is usually found on the hands of those who have a great appreciation for the artistic and beautiful life.

Unlike the major lines, the sun line can come and go, depending upon one's circumstances. If you learn to watch and read your palm on a regular basis, you may discover that the sun line appears at times when you are entering a more visible period in your career or endeavors.

Quality of the sun line
A long, deep sun line belongs to someone who appears larger than life. You waltz into a room. You never leave, or enter, quietly. You surround yourself with beautiful things and have a tendency toward over spending. You are the dazzlers of the world, the entertainers among us.

Meshing or islands on the sun line diffuse this quality somewhat. Often meshing appears on the sun line of those who hang around the stars basking in their glory. These people are less likely to seek fame for themselves. Rather they absorb it through their associations with others.

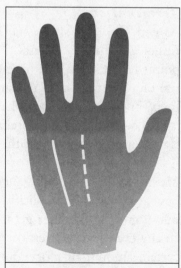

FIG. 17. SUN (FAME) LINE

Origination

A sun line that originates from your life line is the sign of a "star" whose talents were discovered early in childhood and who was pushed or encouraged by family.

If your sun line branches from your fate line, it is a sign of fame coming to you by way of your career.

When your sun line originates from the head line, your fame is hard-earned and usually comes from lengthy intellectual pursuits such as authoring a book, developing a theory or invention, or political prominence.

Finally, if your sun line arises from the heart line, it is a sign of fame in connection with a romantic attachment. This fame may be short lived, as in the case of the lover of a famous person. The prominence often comes from a marriage relationship.

Termination

As with most lines, the sun line is also interpreted by the finger at which it points. For example, when your line points to Mercury, you have gained your fame through the use of a silver tongue. You are the orators, comedians, and mega-buck salespeople of the world. As the Mercury finger is also an indicator of material success, this is oftentimes a sign of great financial wealth.

Most people live happy and contented lives without the benefit of fame or publicity. There is, in fact, a legitimate question as to whether great fame is a blessing or a curse. In any event, the possession of a sun line always indicates a certain amount of glory, publicity, and fame. People with this line on their hands are unlikely to live their lives in total obscurity.

Do you have a sun line?

_____

Is it deep or faint? Does it have meshing or islands? What does this mean to you?

_____

_____

Where does your sun line originate? What does this say?

_____

_____

Where does your sun line terminate? What does this mean?

_____

_____

Does this interpretation seem correct to you? Have you seen the effects of fame on your life?

_____

_____

_____

Lines of affection

The lines of affection, also called the marriage and children lines, often generate a great deal of interest. Unfortunately, they also seem to be the most commonly misinterpreted.

In my opinion, hand analysis is not an effective system of fortune telling. Rather, it tells of your character and personality and, to a certain extent, it tells of the happenings in your life. The lines of affection can, therefore, tell some tales of your past love history, but they are so often misinterpreted that I am tempted not to mention them. There is no one who can tell you when, where, and how love or children will come to you. That is up to you to determine. The most that can be ascertained by looking at your lines of affection is the story of your history of relationships and, more importantly, your ability to relate to others.

Marriage lines in palmistry are the short horizontal lines under your little finger on the mount of Mercury. Fig. 18 shows the approximate location of the lines of affection.

A number of short feathery lines indicates a number of short, rather unserious affairs of the heart. Longer, deeper lines are indicative of more important steady relationships. These lines are read from the heart line up, so that the lines nearest your little finger are affairs or loves in the more recent past.

It is not uncommon to find a hand with only one deep line. This is a sign that you settled early into a serious relationship and have made a long-term commitment to this relationship. Individuals with this line are very monogamous. If you have a large number of lines, you have had, or are more likely to have, a number of affairs prior to or even during a primary relationship.

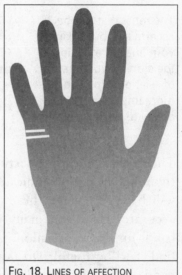

When the affection lines end in a fork, the classic meaning is that the relationship will end in divorce. Once again, however, I stress that this method is not to be used as a prediction technique. If your line ends in a fork and you

Fig. 18. Lines of affection

are still married, it means that you may feel some conflict in your relationship. Look to and address this conflict, and the fork may narrow to a single line.

The lines of affection really do not tell as much about your relationships as they tell about your inclination toward relationships. Read as such, they can provide you with some valuable information about the way you view romantic love.

Persons with strong straight lines of affection have a wish for long and steady love interests. Those with many small lines on their hands tend to have more desire for impermanent unions or affairs.

If your affection lines are wavy, you may be vacillating in regard to commitment and love. Once you have decided on commitment, your affection lines will deepen and straighten.

The most that can be ascertained by looking at your lines of affection is the story of your history of relationships and, more importantly, your ability to relate to others.

Islands on the lines of affection generally indicate that your relationship has reached a point of difficulty and that you are "stuck" in some fashion. These islands will disappear when the difficulty is resolved.

The vertical lines intersecting these lines of affection are traditionally said to indicate the number of children you will have. I believe these "children lines" are very inaccurate. However, many people enjoy searching their hands for this information. If you use this for fun, you may find it to be useful. Do not be upset or disappointed in hand analysis if the children lines are inaccurate. In the twentieth century, the number of children a person has is generally in the control of that person. It is seldom foretold on the palm.

Analyze your lines of affection, keeping in mind that these lines are not, in my opinion, completely accurate in their predictive ability.

How many "marriage lines" do you have on your hand? How many major relationships have you had? Do these agree?

_____

_____

_____

Does your major affection line end in a fork? Are you currently re-evaluating an important relationship?

_____

_____

Are your affection lines straight or wavy? What does this mean?

_____

_____

_____

Do you have islands on your lines of affection?

_____

_____

Do you have "children" lines? Is this accurate for you?

_____

_____

Has the analysis of your lines of affection been helpful?
Why or why not?

_____

_____

_____

Health Line

The line of health starts at the base of your thumb and runs
to below your Mercury finger, forming a triangle with the
head and life lines. This triangle is sometimes called the
lucky triangle and traditional palmists believe that the
greater the area of this triangle, the luckier the life.

It looks something like that in Fig. 19.

The label "health line" is something of a misnomer. When
it is missing, it indicates that you have no significant health
problems at the present time.

It has been my experience that the presence and character
of this line is quite indicative of certain physical ailments.

When your health line is wavy and broken, you are likely to
be suffering from poor health, particularly from nervous
disorders and digestive problems. An island on this line is

likely to mean a hospitaliza-tion. The darker and clearer this line appears on your hand, the more recent have been your health problems. Faint, straight health lines generally indicate that your health disorders have corrected themselves.

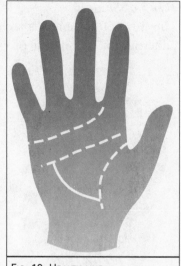

FIG. **19.** HEALTH LINE

Like so many of the secondary lines, this line will come and go with the state of your physical and emotional well-being. If you have a significant health line at the present time, you should take it as a sign that you need to take very good care of yourself. This line often appears in the hands of people who push themselves too hard to accomplish their goals and therefore sacrifice their health for their careers or aspirations.

Do you have a health line?

_____

What is its character?

_____

_____

113

Ring of Solomon

The Ring of Solomon is a circular line that runs along the underside of the mount of your Jupiter finger. This ring is

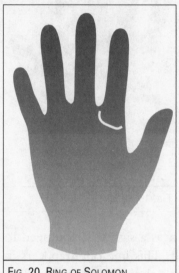

named after a mythical ring owned by King Solomon that allowed him to talk to the birds and animals and that gave him great wisdom. Consequently, possessors of this ring are said to have strong psychic powers and mystic tendencies.

If you have a Ring of Solomon it would look something like Fig. 20.

FIG. 20. RING OF SOLOMON

In my experience, people with this ring express a great deal of interest in psychic phenomena and have a high degree of empathy for their fellows. If you have the ring of Solomon on your hand, you have an inherent talent for understanding others. The deeper and clearer this ring appears, the stronger your mystic connection. Often this ring is quite faint and may be broken or fragmented. This is a sign that your mystical evolution is not complete.

The deeper and clearer this ring appears, the stronger your mystic connection.

Often the Ring of Solomon is found in those who work as counselors and therapists. You have a high degree of understanding of others which generally has a psychic element to it. I consider this line to be very fortunate. Like all other lines, though, it carries its burdens. You may be so sensitive to the feelings of others that you can feel overwhelmed when you are in a crowd of people or when you are in the presence of others with psychological or emotional difficulties.

If you have the Ring of Solomon, you should be aware that you may be overly empathetic. You need to shelter yourself from high-energy circumstances, and you may need to retreat from very populated places. You have a high need to recharge your psychic energy on a regular basis. If you do not recharge, you may find yourself becoming ill as your body forces you to slow down and isolate yourself from others.

Do you have the Ring of Solomon?

What is its character, i.e., deep, broken, faint?

Does this seem correct to you? Why or why not?

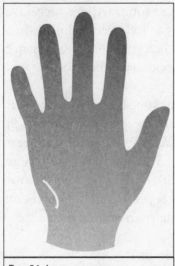

FIG. 21. LINE OF INTUITION

Line of intuition

The line of intuition is an important indicator of psychic capacity and is not present in every hand. It is a semi-circle that runs on the outer edge of the palm. It looks something like Fig. 21.

Your intuition line may cross the health line or even run along it for a time. Do not be upset if you do not have the line of intuition. It is found in the hands of those of you who are highly intuitive about other people. Unfortunately, you often do not have the same intuitive nature about yourself. If you have this line, you are able to know a great deal about people through other than normal means. You are less able to know about yourself (which is why the use of this book should be very valuable for you).

Sometimes this line is broken or incomplete. This is a sign that you have not totally developed your ability, probably because you do not completely trust it. Believe in yourself and in your intuition. Act on your feelings about other people. If you have this line, it is a clear sign that you are intuitive and have strong psychic tendencies. When you have fully embraced this part of yourself, your line of intuition will darken and complete itself.

It is my belief that we all have intuitive capabilities far exceeding anything of which we could ever dream. Trust in these abilities and put them into action. Then watch for your line of intuition to appear.

Do you have a line of intuition?

_____

What is its character?

_____

Does this feel right to you?

_____

_____

_____

Girdle of Venus

The girdle of Venus is a semicircular line between your Saturn and Apollo fingers or occasionally between your Saturn and Mercury fingers. Like all the secondary lines, it does not appear on all hands. When it does, it indicates that you are highly sensitive and often appear to be "high strung." A very dark and deep girdle of Venus shows that you have great depth of feeling, and can sometimes indicate that you possess more than an average amount of physical lust.

It looks something like that illustrated in Fig. 22.

A long, clearly-marked line reaching to the Mercury finger generally belongs to a person who thrives on excitement and thrills. If you have a clear girdle of Venus, you may

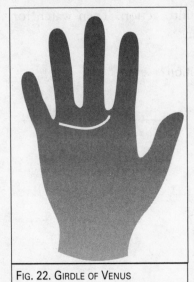

FIG. 22. GIRDLE OF VENUS

wish to consciously moderate your use of alcohol and avoid all types of drugs, as a person with this mark has a higher-than-normal chance of becoming addicted to these substances. You should also be aware that sexual addiction is a possibility.

A short girdle bridging the Saturn and Apollo fingers is a more moderate sign. The owner of such a girdle is sensitive and sexy but not usually excessive. Owners of the girdle of Venus, no matter how faint or deep, seldom have simple love lives.

Do you have a girdle of Venus?

_____

Where is it located—between which fingers?

_____

What is its character—long, deep, faint, etc?

_____

What does this say about you?

_____

Does this seem true?

_____

_____

_____

Travel lines

Travel lines are short horizontal lines on the edge of
the palm opposite the thumb.
They look something like
Fig. 23.

If you have travel lines, you
are sure to possess some
degree of wanderlust, have a
love of adventure and a desire
to see the world.

If you have only one well-
defined travel line, it is an
indication that you will, at

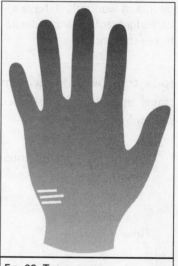

FIG. 23. TRAVEL LINES

some time, change your home location, generally moving
to another state, perhaps to another country. Once settled,
however, you will be content to stay in one place.

Possession of many travel lines is a sign of wanderlust and
love of travel. If you have these lines, you probably crave
the open road, the new land, and the adventure of visiting
foreign places. You may not actually be able to physically
visit all of these worlds, but you have been there in your
dreams. You like to watch travel shows and read about

strange and wonderful places. If you have these lines but have not acted on these urges, you should try to schedule some type of trip into your life. Be careful though, as the travel bug is highly addictive for you.

If you have travel lines, you are sure to possess some degree of wanderlust, have a love of adventure and a desire to see the world.

Sometimes travel lines are crossed by vertical lines or crosses. This can indicate fear of flying or travel. Some palmists believe that it is a prediction of travel accidents. I do not see this to be true, but I do recommend caution in traveling if your travel lines change to reflect new vertical lines prior to a scheduled journey.

Do you have travel lines?

_____

How many?

_____

Are they crossed by vertical lines or crosses?

_____

What does this say about you?

_____

_____

_____

120

Quadrangle

The quadrangle is the term for the space between the heart and head lines. In an average hand the distance between these two lines is about one centimeter.

If your head and heart line run close to parallel to each other, with about one centimeter of distance between them the entire time, you are likely to have an even temper, be mellow in disposition, and have a good sense of humor. People with such an even quadrangle also tend to live life in an even and steady manner.

When the quadrangle is narrower than average, it is a sign of a lack of a sense of humor and imagination. The head and heart line are very close to each other and you tend to "think too much" without using your instinctive senses.

A wider-than-average quadrangle, on the other hand, is possessed by people who perhaps think too little. You tend to be gullible and easily led, and find yourself in trouble without quite knowing why.

If your quadrangle is wider at one end than at the other, you may suffer from some imbalance in your life. People with a wider angle under their Jupiter finger than under their Mercury finger tend to be very ambitious, but may be living this ambition to an extreme. There is a risk of "burning out" and suffering from extreme physical and mental exhaustion.

Conversely, if your quadrangle is wider at the Mercury finger than at the Jupiter finger, you are prone to depression. You have the possibility of being immobilized by your emotional state and may become unable to handle the affairs of life.

A waisted quadrangle, wide at both ends, is the hand of a worrier. If your quadrangle is waisted, you are probably familiar with insomnia and need to learn to "let go" of life and its problems.

Nearly everyone's quadrangle has some sort of angle at one end. This is not to be taken as a significant cause for concern. Rather, you merely need to be aware of your vulnerability and protect yourself as best as you can. For example, if you know that you are prone to depression, you will be on guard for its symptoms and take action prior to suffering its full immobilizing effects.

What does this mean to you?

_____

_____

_____

Is this true in terms of your emotional reaction to stressful times?

_____

_____

_____

_____

Psychic Cross

The quadrangle is the location for the psychic, or mystic, cross. The psychic cross is an "X" or cross in the middle of the quadrangle, and is a sign of clear vision or mystical awareness. Possession of the psychic cross usually indicates that you have an interest in, although not necessarily a strong talent for, psychic and mystical phenomena. The psychic cross looks like Fig. 24.

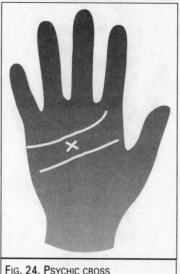

FIG. 24. PSYCHIC CROSS

Possessors of the psychic cross need to act with some care in their pursuit of the mystical. While you have great interest, you also tend to be vulnerable to the charlatans that occasionally prey on you. Particularly if your quadrangle is wider than normal, you tend to

> Possessors of the psychic cross need to act with some care in their pursuit of the mystical.

be somewhat gullible and need to learn to always ask yourself if what you are hearing feels right to you. Never give away your power to know what's best for you.

Teacher's Square

The teacher's square is a small square located between the heart and head lines directly under the Jupiter finger. It looks like Fig. 25.

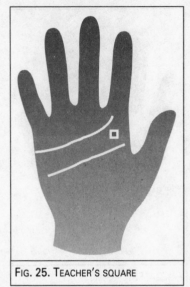

FIG. 25. TEACHER'S SQUARE

If you have a teacher's square on your hand, you have a talent for teaching, lecturing or instructing. You may or may not actually be a teacher, as many people with this square are not utilizing their gift. Also, many truly gifted teachers have left the teaching profession in frustration with the system. However, this sign is a clear indication of the ability to instruct. Be aware of this ability if you have it as you can use it in many of life's endeavors.

Do you have the Psychic Cross?

_____

Do you have the teacher's square?

_____

What does this mean to you?

_____

_____

_____

_____

124

Poison line

The so-called poison line is a short, horizontal line or bar located low on the Mount of Luna, at the edge of the palm opposite the thumb. It looks something like Fig. 26.

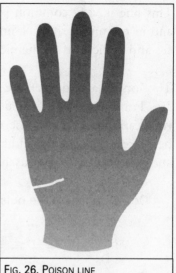

FIG. 26. POISON LINE

Possession of the poison line is, in my opinion, a reliable indicator of a person who is highly susceptible to the effects of various chemicals, poisons, and drugs. It is also found in a significant number of people who suffer from allergies. I have been impressed with the reliability of this line and wonder about its value to the medical community. Perhaps someday hand analysis will be used by doctors as another diagnostic tool. Until such time, you can be aware of your susceptibility, and take precautions on your own.

If you have the poison line on your hand, you will react unusually to medication and chemicals. You may need more than a usual dose to get an effect, or on the contrary, you may react violently to a small dosage. Children with this line have a susceptibility to hyperactivity and react drastically to sugar and caffeine. Adults with this line have a tendency to develop addictions to just about any chemical they ingest, particularly nicotine, alcohol, caffeine, and all mood-altering drugs.

> If you have the poison line on your hand, you will react unusually to medication and chemicals.

This line is very common in the "recovering" community, and in my mind, shows a link between allergies to substances and addictions to chemicals.

The longer and deeper the line, the more susceptible you are. For this reason, if you possess this line, you must be very careful about the use of any medication. You should be extremely careful handling chemicals such as pesticides and other hazardous household products.

Do you possess the poison line?

_____

Do you suffer from allergies?

_____

Have you been troubled by addiction to any chemical or drug?

_____

_____

_____

_____

13

Putting It All Together

Using all the bits and pieces you have learned about yourself, it is now time to put those pieces together.

Use these pages to write a brief summary of what you have learned about yourself, and your opinion of the accuracy of this information.

From analyzing my thumb I learned that I:

_____

_____

_____

My fingers show that I:

_____

_____

_____

My heart line indicates:

_____

_____

_____

I learned from my head line that I:

_____

_____

_____

My life line says:

_____

_____

_____

According to my fate line I:

_____

_____

_____

I have a sun line. This means that I:

_____

_____

_____

My lines of affection told me this:

_____

_____

_____

I have a health line. This means that I:

_____

_____

_____

I possess the Ring of Solomon. It means I:

_____

_____

_____

My line of intuition tells me:

_____

_____

I have a girdle of Venus. This means:

_____

_____

_____

My travel lines mean:

_____

_____

_____

I learned this from examining my quadrangle:

_____

_____

_____

I have a psychic cross which means:

_____

_____

_____

Possessing a teacher's square means that I:

_____

_____

_____

The poison line on my palm means that I should:

_____

_____

_____

Use this space to write any final remarks about the process of hand analysis and your response to it.

_____

_____

_____

_____

_____

_____

_____

_____

_____

_____

_____

14

In Closing

My hope is that you have had fun in this process, and that you also have learned a little something new about yourself at the same time. Do not dwell on the personality characteristics you possess that you consider to be negative. It is much more important to emphasize those qualities you have that you consider to be positive. You are a unique and special individual with a wonderful mixture of personality traits. The most important thing for you is to become aware of who you are so that you can be fully yourself.

Remember that just as all living things grow and change, so do you. The lines on your palm and structure of your hand will grow and change also. Use the skills you have developed in doing this workbook to track the path on which you travel, rejoicing always in the journey.

Glossary

An Alphabetical Guide To Terms

AFFECTION LINES: Small horizontal lines on the outside of the palm, under the little finger. Each line is said to indicate a romantic relationship. Vertical lines intersecting with these lines may be used as a predictor or indicator for the number of children which a person may have.

AGING A LINE: Using the lines to approximate at what time in one's life an occurrence happened. Aging is not an exact science, but it can aid in determining when certain events happened in one's past.

APOLLO FINGER: The third finger from the thumb, commonly known as the ring finger. A well-developed Apollo finger is indicative of an artistic and spiritual nature.

BRANCHES: A line continuing in a different direction from another line. It often indicates a new direction or change in one's life.

BREAK: When a line stops completely. This is generally considered to indicate a new start or a crisis in one's life.

CHAIN: A series of circles or islands chained together along a line. A chain on a line usually indicates weakness or difficulties.

CLUBBED THUMB OR FINGER: The top phalange of the thumb or finger is heavy and thick, taking the shape of a club. To be clubbed, the thumb or finger must show a very exaggerated thickness.

CROSS: Two intersecting lines appearing either on the palm or along a line. It often indicates a struggle or battle occurring in one's life.

DOMINANT HAND: The hand which is most often used; generally the hand which is used for writing and which is the strongest hand. This hand will show the destiny and character which has been created by a person's life experiences.

FATE LINE: The line which runs vertically up the palm from the middle of the base of the palm to the area of the Saturn finger. It often indicates one's ideal career and should be read by examining the characteristics of the finger to which it is pointing.

FORK: A fork at the beginning or end of a line indicates that the person is in a period of decision making and is approaching a change in his or her life.

GRID OR GRILLE: A crossing of horizontal and vertical lines. It is generally a sign of problems or dilemmas in one's life.

GIRDLE OF VENUS: A semi-circle linking the Saturn and Apollo fingers. This line is sometimes broken or incomplete. It indicates great depth of feeling, including a possible over-emphasis on sexual matters.

HEAD LINE: One of the three major lines of the palm. It starts at the inside of the palm above the thumb and life line and runs horizontally across the palm. It indicates one's method of thinking.

HEART LINE: A major line of the palm which runs horizontally across the palm from the base of the Mercury finger. It indicates one's method of love and romantic relationships.

HEALTH LINE: A minor line which does not occur on every hand. It runs diagonally across the palm, connecting the life and head lines. Its presence indicates some health problems of a past or current nature.

INTUITION LINE: A curved line starting at the outer base of the palm and curving upward to the outer edge of the palm beneath the Mercury finger. It is present only on the hands of those people with a strong ability to understand and empathize with other people.

ISLAND: An oval or circular marking on a line which usually indicates a blockage of some type.

JUPITER FINGER: The first finger from the thumb, also known as the index finger. A well-developed Jupiter finger is an indicator of ambition, leadership ability, and high ego-strength.

KNOTTY FINGERS: A knotty finger is one in which the knuckle is very pronounced. If the knuckles are not large and pronounced, the finger is considered to be smooth. It is possible to have both knotty and smooth fingers on one hand.

LIFE LINE: A major line of the palm which starts on the inside of the palm between the thumb and Jupiter finger and curves down the hand to the middle of the base of the palm. It is an indicator of life force and vitality.

MERCURY FINGER: The name given to the little finger of the hand. It is an indicator of communication skills and sexuality.

MOUNTS: Mounts are the cushioned or padded areas directly underneath the fingers and on the sides of the palm. When they are well-developed or poorly-developed, they reveal information about the traits which are governed by the fingers above them.

MYSTIC CROSS: A cross in the quadrangle, the area between the heart and head lines. Possession of the mystic cross shows psychic ability or interest.

NON-DOMINANT HAND: Generally, the weaker and less used hand. This hand will reflect a person's potential and character as it could have been prior to being shaped by life's experiences.

PHALANGES: The divided segments of the fingers and the thumb. Each finger and the thumb has three phalanges, which can be seen on the inside of the palm only. The phalanges are measured from the bottom line of one phalange to the bottom line of the next.

POISON LINE: A short horizontal line on the edge of the palm across from the thumb but above the travel lines. A reliable indicator of susceptibility to various chemicals, including drugs and alcohol and/or a high likelihood of allergies.

QUADRANGLE: The area between the head and heart lines is called the quadrangle. The shape of the quadrangle shows one's method of dealing with stress and anxiety. The mystic cross is found in the quadrangle.

RING OF SOLOMON: A curved line circling the Jupiter finger. It indicates mystical and psychic interest and an uncommon ability to understand other people.

SATURN FINGER: The middle finger of the hand is called the Saturn finger. It represents balance and wisdom.

SECONDARY LINES: Any line on one's palm which is not the head, heart or life line is a secondary line. Everyone does not have every secondary line and no one has all the secondary lines. Do not be concerned if you do not have every line mentioned in this book.

SPATULATE: A spatulate finger is spade-shaped with the tip being broader than the base of the finger.

SUN LINE: The line which runs vertically up the palm from the base of the palm to the area of the Apollo finger. This line does not appear on all hands, but when it does it indicates that a certain amount of fame will occur to the person. It is also called the fame or Apollo line.

TEACHER'S SQUARE: A small square located under the Jupiter finger between the heart and head lines. Possession of this square indicates talent for teaching, lecturing or instructing.

THUMB: The thumb of the hand is related to one's will and is an indicator of one's ego strength and character. The thumb is sometimes called Rhea in traditional palmistry.

TRAVEL LINES: Short horizontal lines on the edge of the palm opposite the thumb. They are a sign of wander-lust and a love of travel and adventure.

Index

M

Manipulative, 31
Major lines, 3, 56, 57, 60, 62, 65, 91, 97, 105
Marriage, 108, 109, 111
Mercury finger, 51-55, 65, 104, 106, 112, 121
Mesh, 4, 60, 63, 74-75, 81, 83, 86, 91, 105, 107
Mobility, 20, 29, 33
Moral, 41, 42, 79
Mount of Apollo, 48-49
Mount of Jupiter, 38-39
Mount of Mercury, 53-54
Mount of Saturn, 43-44
Mount of Venus, 30-33, 88, 89
Murderer's thumb, 31, 32
Mystic, 93, 114, 123

N

Nails, 14, 17, 18, 19, 21
Netting, 60, 62, 67, 75, 81
Non-dominant hand, 6, 7, 25, 37, 43, 53, 58, 73, 83, 90, 98-99

O

Originality, 49

P

Perspiring hands, 16
Phalanges, 8-9, 13, 25-26, 32
Poison line, 125-126, 131
Prediction, 59, 102, 109, 120

Psychic ability, 47, 64, 87, 114, 115, 116, 123-124
Psychic cross, 123, 124, 131

Q

Quadrangle, 121-122, 130

R

Rage, 31, 70
Rebel, 53, 82
Relationships, 27, 36, 37, 51, 54, 63, 65-67, 69, 71, 79, 80, 106, 109-110
Resilience, 38
Respiratory disorder, 18
Rigid, 14, 20-21
Ring of Solomon, 114-115, 129
Rhea, 25
Romance, 54, 67-68, 70, 106, 109

S

Saturn finger, 16, 35-37, 41-45, 65-66, 79, 100, 117
Secondary lines, 16, 97-126,
Secretive, 19, 52, 53
Self-employed, 100
Self-esteem, 36, 52, 54
Self-revealing, 19, 20, 28-29
Sensuality, 26
Sexuality, 26, 51, 53, 54, 79, 118
Shallow lines, 58, 74, 75, 87

Index